CAREERS IN SCIENCE AND ENGINEERING

A STUDENT PLANNING GUIDE TO GRAD SCHOOL AND BEYOND

Committee on Science, Engineering, and Public Policy

NATIONAL ACADEMY OF SCIENCES
NATIONAL ACADEMY OF ENGINEERING
INSTITUTE OF MEDICINE

NATIONAL ACADEMY PRESS
Washington, D.C.   1996

National Academy Press • 2101 Constitution Ave., N.W. • Washington, DC 20418

NOTICE: This volume was produced as part of a project approved by the Governing Board of the National Research Council, whose members are drawn from the councils of the National Academy of Sciences, the National Academy of Engineering, and the Institute of Medicine. It is a result of work done by the Committee on Science, Engineering, and Public Policy (COSEPUP) as augmented, which has authorized its release to the public. This report has been reviewed by a group other than the authors according to procedures approved by COSEPUP and the Report Review Committee.

Financial Support: The development of this guide was supported by the Arthur L. Day Fund of the National Academy of Sciences. Support for the dissemination of this guide was provided by the Burroughs Wellcome Fund, Shell Oil Company Foundation, Glaxo Wellcome Inc., Bristol-Myers Squibb Pharmaceutical Research Institute, Philips Research, and the following disciplinary societies: American Chemical Society, American Institute of Physics, American Mathematical Society, Society for Industrial and Applied Mathematics, American Sociological Association, American Association of Medical Colleges, American Psychological Association, American Geophysical Union, Geological Society of America, American Society for Cell Biology, American Astronomical Society, National Consortium for Graduate Degrees for Minorities in Science and Engineering, American Geological Institute, Sigma Xi, the Federation of American Societies for Experimental Biology, the American Society for Microbiology, the American Institute for Biological Sciences, and the American Physical Society.

Internet Access: This report is available on the National Academy of Sciences' Internet host. It may be accessed via World Wide Web at http://www.nas.edu, via Gopher at gopher.nas.edu, or via FTP at ftp.nas.edu.

Cover illustration by Leigh Coriale.

Printed in the United States of America

PROJECT GUIDANCE GROUP

ARDEN L. BEMENT (*Chair*), Basil S. Turner Distinguished Professor of Engineering, Purdue University

DAVID R. CHALLONER, Vice President for Health Affairs, University of Florida

ELLIS B. COWLING, University Distinguished Professor At-Large, North Carolina State University

GERALD P. DINNEEN, Retired Vice President, Science and Technology, Honeywell, Inc.

PHILLIP A. GRIFFITHS, Director, Institute for Advanced Study

RUBY P. HEARN, Vice President, The Robert Wood Johnson Foundation

PHILLIP A. SHARP, Head, Department of Biology, Center for Cancer Research, Massachusetts Institute of Technology

Principal Project Staff

DEBORAH D. STINE, Associate Director for Special Projects
TAMAE M. WONG, Senior Program Officer
ALAN ANDERSON, Consultant-Writer
NORMAN GROSSBLATT, Editor
PATRICK P. SEVCIK, Project Assistant

The **National Academy of Sciences** (NAS) is a private, nonprofit, self-perpetuating society of distinguished scholars engaged in scientific and engineering research, dedicated to the furtherance of science and technology and to their use for the general welfare. Under the authority of the charter granted to it by Congress in 1863, the Academy has a working mandate that calls on it to advise the federal government on scientific and technical matters. Dr. Bruce M. Alberts is president of the NAS.

The **National Academy of Engineering** (NAE) was established in 1964, under the charter of the NAS, as a parallel organization of distinguished engineers. It is autonomous in its administration and in the selection of members, sharing with the NAS its responsibilities for advising the federal government. The National Academy of Engineering also sponsors engineering programs aimed at meeting national needs, encourages education and research, and recognizes the superior achievements of engineers. Dr. Harold Liebowitz is president of the NAE.

The **Institute of Medicine** (IOM) was established in 1970 by the NAS to secure the services of eminent members of appropriate professions in the examination of policy matters pertaining to the health of the public. The Institute acts under the responsibility given to the NAS in its congressional charter to be an adviser to the federal government and, on its own initiative, to identify issues of medical care, research, and education. Dr. Kenneth I. Shine is president of the IOM.

The **Committee on Science, Engineering, and Public Policy** (COSEPUP) is a joint committee of the NAS, the NAE, and the IOM. It includes current and former members of the councils of all three bodies.

PREFACE

This guide is intended to help upper-division under-graduate and graduate students in science, engineering, and mathematics to make career and educational choices.

Although it is understandable that students, particularly at the graduate level, identify with their faculty mentors and often aspire to academic research careers, education in science and engineering can be extremely valuable for a wide variety of career opportunities. Some of those careers involve direct participation in science or engineering—for example, as a chemist or engineer in industry or as a professional who performs research and development. Many others involve using a science and engineering background. For example, one might teach about science and engineering in schools or through the media or provide advice or develop policies on matters relevant to science or engineering. Each of these activities is a legitimate and valuable use of a science or engineering background.

We need not focus on the *doing* of science and engineering as the only appropriate sequel to advanced study. To do so implicitly (and sometimes explicitly) has the effect of devaluing other career goals and excluding potentially important experiences from our education programs. The report *Reshaping the Graduate Education of Scientists and Engineers* (1995), by the Committee on Science, Engineering, and Public Policy (COSEPUP) of the National Academy of Sciences (NAS), National Academy of Engineering (NAE), and Institute of Medicine (IOM), demonstrates that students need flexible career preparation and urges a re-evaluation of graduate education so that it will prepare students better for productive careers. Discussions during the preparation and dissemination of that report indicated the need for a guide designed specifically to help students to plan their educational and professional careers. This guide is a result of those discussions. It seeks to assist students in taking a much broader view of the potential applications of their science and engineering education.

It is supplemented by the Internet *Career Planning Center For Beginning Scientists and Engineers*, which can be reached via the Academies' homepage at **http://www2. nas.edu/cpc**. At this online career-planning center, students will find up-to-date guidance and information, including a bulletin board where they can ask questions and seek advice about their education or career, a one-on-one mentoring program, lists of specific employment opportunities, education and career analysis focused on students' questions, and sources of more discipline- and occupation-specific information. An online version of this guide can also be obtained at the center.

Which Sections Are For You?

Different parts of this student guide will help students at different stages of their career and education. You might want to skip through the guide to sections that are most relevant to you.

Secondary-school students and undecided undergraduates can use the guide to help them to understand careers in science and engineering and to find practical tips on how to proceed.

Undergraduate students currently studying science and engineering can use this guide to decide what careers they are interested in pursuing (Chapter 2), evaluate their skills and attributes (Chapter 3), and determine whether they need additional graduate education or a professional education. If they decide to pursue graduate education in science or engineering, Chapter 4 will help them to select a graduate school and major.

Beginning graduate students will have made many of the educational choices described in Chapter 4, but the material on advisors, research topics, achieving breadth, and ensuring progress should be of interest.

Chapters 2, 3, and 5 will also be of use for more-experienced students. Like those who are approaching the end of their undergraduate education, students approaching the end of their graduate studies will want to evaluate their careers and their personal skills and attributes as they decide what to do during the next stage of their lives. Some students will be interested in pursuing a career immediately; others will want additional graduate or professional education or post-doctoral appointments.

Students who have already chosen their careers might still find this guide valuable. The guide emphasizes personal flexibility and broad education. It also provides sources of information that students can use in evaluating the potential job market in a chosen area. A sizable fraction of even the most dedicated students will not necessarily find a career in their chosen occupation and should be prepared to look elsewhere.

The guide also seeks to be helpful to those who administer graduate programs and to faculty members and others who advise students. Graduate students need more and better information about careers, and faculty advisers can play an important role in supplying it.

Although this guide is brief and informal, it is designed to be useful throughout your career. The information in it should be relevant to students interested not only in research careers, but in other science-oriented careers as well.

Where Do the Information and Guidance Come From?

The content of this guide was shaped by information gathered from focus groups and surveys of students and postdoctoral appointees. The surveys revealed students' desire for additional help in answering such questions as the following:

➤ Should I go to graduate school, and where?

➤ Where can I get advice about different disciplines?

➤ What type of experience should I obtain beyond my formal classwork?

➤ What classes should I take outside my major?

➤ Should I stop at the master's level or pursue a PhD?

➤ What should be the relationship between me and my research adviser?

➤ How my career goals affect my choice of thesis topic?

➤ What nonresearch skills do I need, and how do I attain them?

➤ Is a postdoctoral experience desirable for me?

➤ How much salary will I make when I graduate? Is it worth the investment in time and opportunity cost?

Students also expressed a need for career guidance information on

➤ Identifying careers.

➤ Educational requirements for various careers.

➤ Off-campus and postgraduate research and education (extramural programs).

➤ Skills and attributes that could improve employment options.

Addressing issues like these is fundamental to a satisfying professional career. In these pages, we encourage students to seek help from peers, friends, advisers, and many other sources in planning a career in science and engineering. It is true that you, the student, are finally responsible for shaping your own career, but your success is largely a product of the abundance and accuracy of career information and the guidance of those familiar with the world beyond graduate school.

Preparation of this guide, a companion publication to COSEPUP's other student guide, *On Being a Scientist: Responsible Conduct in Research* (1995), was overseen by a guidance group consisting of Arden Bement (chair), David Challoner, Ellis Cowling, Ralph Gomory, M.R.C. Greenwood, Phillip Griffiths, Ruby Hearn, Gerald Dinneen, and Phillip Sharp. The group was aided by early reviews of its guide by an external advisory group consisting of graduate students and professors, members of science and engineering disciplinary societies and organizations, and focus groups of graduate and postgraduate students. Staff for the project included Deborah Stine, associate director for special projects for COSEPUP; Alan Anderson, science writer; and Tamae Maeda Wong, senior program officer.

BRUCE M. ALBERTS
President, National Academy of Sciences

HAROLD LIEBOWITZ
President, National Academy of Engineering

KENNETH I. SHINE
President, Institute of Medicine

ACKNOWLEDGMENTS

The committee thanks particularly its external advisory group, who provided valuable guidance throughout the development of this guide:

MARY R. ANDERSON-ROWLAND, Associate Dean of Student Affairs and Special Programs, College of Engineering and Applied Science, Arizona State University

RICHARD ATTIYEH, Office of Graduate Studies and Research, University of California, San Diego

ANDREW G. EWING, Professor of Chemistry, Pennsylvania State University

EDWIN GOLDIN, Manager, Career Planning and Placement, American Institute of Physics

CATHARINE E. JOHNSON, Graduate Student, Department of Biological Chemistry, Johns Hopkins School of Medicine

IRENE KENNEDY, Career Consultant and former Manager, FASEB Career Resources

PETER A. LEWIS, Managing Director, Educational Activities, The Institute of Electrical and Electronics Engineers, Inc.

PETER SYVERSON, Vice President for Research and Information Services, Council of Graduate Schools

EDEL WASSERMAN, Science Advisor, Central Research and Development, E.I. du Pont de Nemours & Co.

CRYSTAL WILLIAMS, Graduate Student, Department of Chemistry, Louisiana State University

In addition, the committee thanks the students of Johns Hopkins University in Baltimore, Maryland, the University of California, Irvine, and Georgetown University in Washington, D.C., who participated in focus-group sessions and students at Yale University and Florida State University who commented on early drafts. All provided invaluable suggestions on earlier drafts of the guide.

Special thanks also go to the individuals who agreed to be profiled in this report: Carol Balfe, Mary Carol Day, Bill Edge, Mark Ferrari, Diana Garcia-Prichard, Russell Greig, Steve Hays, Janice Hicks, Patricia Hoben, Toby Horn, Resha Putzrath, Rochelle Seide, and Shankar Vedantam.

Finally, the committee thanks its able staff: Deborah Stine, who managed the project, developed background for Chapter 4, and ran the focus groups on the guide; Alan Anderson, science writer, whose help in drafting this guide was invaluable; Tamae Maeda Wong, who developed the background text for Chapter 2 and the profiles; Norman Grossblatt, who edited the report; and Patrick Sevcik, who provided administrative support.

A NOTE ON
USING THIS GUIDE

One theme of this guide is that those studying science and engineering need more information about planning careers than is readily available to them. You need to know more about resources, about what your predecessors have done, and about how to match your own skills and personality to a given career.

In addition to the regular text, this guide offers a variety of learning tools: a series of brief profiles of scientists and engineers, some hypothetical scenarios that illustrate challenges that you might encounter in making decisions about your educational or professional life, and end-of-chapter action points that should be reviewed periodically as you move through the guide.

In the profiles, you might notice that we do not emphasize "traditional" careers—those of scientists and engineers who follow the trajectory of their early work in research positions at universities, industrial laboratories, or government laboratories. One example of a traditional track is the scientist who joins and remains with a single university as an instructor, assistant professor, associate professor, and professor. In fact, only a minority of scientists and engineers follow such paths. Most of the profiles are designed to illustrate the many ways in which scientists and engineers seize new opportunities that shift their careers onto new and unexpected paths. Few of the professionals who are profiled knew during graduate school what they would be doing today. They share a degree of flexibility, breadth, and social skills that allowed them to take advantage of new opportunities.

The scenarios present common dilemmas encountered by graduate students at different stages of their careers. Each dilemma is followed by questions that can serve as the basis of informal discussion or individual pondering. Further discussion of each issue is offered in Appendix A.

Those tools, and the guide itself, are designed for use in many different settings, including

➤ Undergraduate or graduate courses in science and engineering.
➤ University or other career-counseling offices.
➤ Job fairs and conventions.
➤ Student discussion or support groups.
➤ Professional-society meetings.
➤ University orientation sessions.
➤ Faculty adviser–student meetings.
➤ Information interviews.

A useful format in any of these situations is a panel discussion involving several researchers who are at different stages of their careers—for example, an undergraduate, a graduate student, a postdoctoral fellow, a junior faculty member, and a senior faculty member. In addition, representatives of industry, business, or government can add perspective for students who might have little understanding of nonacademic careers.

Most important, we hope to stimulate discussion of a topic that receives insufficient attention. It is our hope that all those who teach, advise, and employ scientists and engineers will become more aware of their responsibilities in guiding students. When young scientists and engineers make good choices about their careers, they contribute more to a society increasingly dependent on their education and skills.

CONTENTS

CAREERS IN SCIENCE
AND ENGINEERING

WHAT ARE YOUR CAREER GOALS?

People seek careers in science or engineering for many reasons. Some have specific goals: they wish to cure diseases or combat hunger or reduce pollution; or they dream of developing the next laser, transistor, or vehicle for space travel; or they imagine building companies that capitalize on new engineering capabilities. Some choose careers in science or engineering because they are curious about the natural world. Others are motivated by the excitement and beauty of the intellectual world and hope to formulate theories that will lead to new ways of thinking about the world. Still others imagine educating people about science or engineering in schools or through the media; they want to provide counsel or shape public policies on issues of direct relevance to science or engineering. Each of these motivations is legitimate, each is valuable, and each flows naturally from an education in science and engineering.

Careers in science and engineering are essentially hope-filled endeavors that can improve people's lives and result in knowledge that all people can share. As the techniques

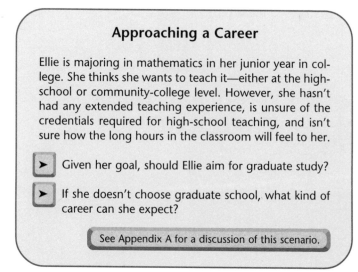

Approaching a Career

Ellie is majoring in mathematics in her junior year in college. She thinks she wants to teach it—either at the high-school or community-college level. However, she hasn't had any extended teaching experience, is unsure of the credentials required for high-school teaching, and isn't sure how the long hours in the classroom will feel to her.

► Given her goal, should Ellie aim for graduate study?

► If she doesn't choose graduate school, what kind of career can she expect?

See Appendix A for a discussion of this scenario.

and products of science and technology have become more central to modern society, a background in science and engineering has become essential to more and more careers. In fact, degrees in science and engineering are becoming as fundamental to modern life as the traditional liberal-arts degree. The contributions of scientists and engineers already extend beyond research and development and throughout the realms of teaching, business, industry, and government. People with bachelor's, master's, and doctoral degrees in science or engineering are forming companies, managing businesses, practicing law, formulating policy, consulting, and running for political office. They are forming global communities of common interests that transcend the differences among individuals, corporate endeavors, or nations.

But if you are contemplating a career in science or engineering, how can you begin your planning most effectively? If you are an undergraduate or beginning graduate student—the groups for whom this guide is primarily de-

How does a GENETICIST/MOLECULAR BIOLOGIST . . .

Get to be a PATENT LAWYER?

Rochelle Karen Seide, who was trained as a biologist, now enjoys a rewarding career as a patent attorney specializing in biotechnology. After beginning her studies in bacteriology and earning a PhD in human genetics, she completed her schooling with a law degree. This seemingly radical career change, she says, came naturally enough—as an extension of her inborn "people" skills.

"Even when I was a scientist [at Northeastern Ohio Universities College of Medicine], I spent a lot of time with other people—teaching, doing genetic counseling. I liked the interpersonal aspects of my work as well as the science. Patent practice lets me use them both."

Dr. Seide is now an attorney in the New York firm of Brumbaugh, Graves, Donohue & Raymond. In her specialty of intellectual-property law, she spends much of her time in litigation and counseling: Does a new biotechnology process or product merit a patent? Can a client expect good protection for the life of the patent? To answer such questions, she must understand the cutting-edge research that her clients are doing. She could not do this without her expertise in—and love for—science.

continued

PATENT LAWYER—*continued*

Dr. Seide feels that it was important to focus on science for its own sake while working toward her PhD. However, she encourages students to understand that "if you want to do science from another perspective, more avenues are open to you. I have found how exciting it is to learn from people in other disciplines and to look at science from other perspectives."

signed—how well do your own skills and personality match the career you imagine?

It is important to remember that science-oriented students are not all alike, any more than all artists or all politicians are alike. Your success will depend on going where your particular interests lead you. Are you exhilarated by the challenge of a new problem or puzzle or need? Does the complexity of the natural world prompt a desire to understand it? If so, science and engineering study—rigorous though it is—will provide you with the tools and concepts that you need to achieve your goals.

Your own goals will determine which academic degree is most appropriate for you. Many people find satisfying careers in a variety of positions after the bachelor's degree. Others, notably engineers, find that a master's degree equips them well for professional careers. For those who hope for careers conducting research and/or teaching at the university level, a PhD will probably be required.

No degree guarantees lifetime employment. Like professionals in other fields, you might still have to change jobs and even careers during your life—perhaps more than once. It is the purpose of this guide to help you lay the foundation for your journey, no matter how many turns your path takes.

Just how rigorous is the path to a scientific or engineering career? Graduate study, in particular, is demanding mentally, physically, and emotionally. Not everyone has the perseverance to complete years of concentrated study. But the experience of doing scientific or technical work is supremely exhilarating for those with sufficient interest and determination. And many people will be willing to help you along the way and assist you over difficult hurdles as you gain the confidence to think and work independently.

Are you bright enough to become a scientist or engineer? Again, there is no standard against which to measure yourself; no kind of intelligence applies across all the many fields of science and engineering. But you can do no better than to trust in your deepest feeling. If your enjoyment of mathematics and science is real, you will probably want to understand, use, and explore them on a deeper level.

One of the most helpful guides to doctoral study in both science and engineering is a slim book by scientist and writer Peter Medawar titled *Advice to a Young Scientist*. Medawar writes: "A novice must stick it out until he [or she] discovers whether the rewards and compensations of a scientific [or engineering] life are for him [or her] commensurate with the disappointments and the toil; but if once a scientist [or engineer] experiences the exhilaration of discovery and the satisfaction of carrying through a really tricky experiment . . . then he [or she] is hooked and no other kind of life will do." And again Medawar is helpful: "One does not need to be terrifically brainy to be a good scientist . . . . Common sense one cannot do without, and one would be the better for owning some of those old-fashioned virtues . . . application, diligence, a sense of purpose, the power to concentrate, to persevere and not be cast down by adversity." (Medawar 1979).

Action Points

▶ Make a list of reasons why you like to study science and engineering and a list of reasons why you don't. Compare the two lists.

▶ Make a list of the positive and negative aspects of various careers in which you are interested.

▶ Seek out people with science and engineering backgrounds who work in careers in which you are interested and ask them to have lunch with you so that you can ask them about their work and how they got where they are today. How do they spend their time? What do they find most satisfying and most disagreeable? Does the life that they describe appeal to you?

▶ If you're an undergraduate, talk with several graduate students; if you're a beginning graduate student, talk with several advanced students or postdoctoral students. Ask them what they have learned that they wish they had known early in their careers.

HOW CAN YOU MEET YOUR CAREER GOALS?

This guide offers advice that might be useful to people at every stage along their career path—from undergraduates wondering "what they would like to be when they grow up" to established professionals pondering a career change. Younger students might not yet confront the challenges of seeking jobs and changing careers, but even undergraduates are well advised to consider a career in science or engineering in its entirety. To emphasize this point, this chapter on defining your career goals comes *before* the ones on skill attainment (Chapter 3) and education (Chapter 4). This gives you an opportunity to focus on your career goals first—and then on what you need to attain those goals.

Envisioning a Career

If you're considering a career in science or engineering, step back and imagine the shape of that career. Do you want to focus on "doing" science or engineering? Or a career that is not necessarily categorized as doing science or engineering but instead uses your science or engineering background to make your contribution to society in a different way? Where would you like to be in 5 years? In 20 years? Can you imagine getting there from where you are today?

If you are like most students, it is highly unlikely that you will find specific answers to career questions before graduating. But it is never too soon to find out as much as you can about yourself and the career you envision, alternatives to that career, and how best to match your own personality and desires with the shape of possible careers in science and engineering.

Planning a Career

Of course, there is a limit to how carefully students can—or should—try to plan for an unknowable future. You might have gained the impression that careers proceed in a more or less straight line that begins with an undergraduate degree and leads directly to the position you anticipated. But most career paths are neither straight nor predictable—nor, in the end, would people want them to be. Careers can have as many sudden turns and new directions as life itself. Even your earliest steps along this path will probably be guided by accidents of timing and opportunity as much as by intention. You will go to a particular school or take a particular position because of a conversation with a friend or adviser or a random bit of news. Or someone on a university admissions committee is attracted by a particular detail in your application. Or a postdoctoral position opens on the same day that you happen to call a friend in the same department. The more you have thought about your career, the better able you will be to take advantage of such unplanned events.

As Louis Pasteur observed, "Chance favors the prepared mind."

That is the nature of careers in science and engineering—as it is of careers in general (Tobias et al. 1995). The profiles that appear throughout this book demonstrate how fluid the course of American education and employment can be when you are sufficiently qualified, motivated, and open-minded to accept a new opportunity when it comes.

How Careers in Science and Engineering Are Changing

Most scientists and engineers find careers in three general sectors of society: colleges and universities, industries, and federal and state agencies. Their work includes an array of activities, from the conduct of basic and applied research to the design and application of new commercial products to the operation and maintenance of large engineering systems.

You can make your planning more effective by appreciating the direction in which professional careers are shifting within that larger picture. For example, for many students, a PhD will mean a career as an academic researcher. But more than half the students who receive PhDs in science and engineering obtain work outside academe—a proportion that has increased steadily for 2 decades. And full-time academic positions in general are more difficult to find than they were during the 1960s and 1970s, when the research enterprise was expanding more rapidly.

As our society changes, so too do the opportunities for careers in science and engineering. The end of the Cold War has removed some incentive for the federal government to fund defense-oriented basic research. Increased national and global competition has forced many industries to reduce expenses and staff. That means that there are fewer research and development positions in universities, industries, and government laboratories than there are qualified scientists and engineers looking for them.

Powerful changes have swept through the universities. For example, there are strong public pressures for universities to shift their emphasis toward teaching and toward undergraduate education; the number of positions for permanent faculty has decreased; professors are no longer required to retire at a particular age; and more part-time and temporary faculty are being employed. All those trends affect the universities' ability to hire scientists and engineers.

At the same time, small and medium-sized companies in some fields are increasing their research and development activity as they develop new technologies. The natural advance of technology is creating new opportunities in information science, software design, biotechnology, data processing, environmental engineering, electronic networking, manufacturing and computational simulation, and forensic science. Government agencies are converting some of their defense-oriented efforts to research in environmental work, communication, information, and other fields. Recent graduates with skills in more than a single discipline are attractive to businesses in these and other multidisciplinary fields, especially if they have dual master's degrees or strong minors (see Chapter 4).

Scientists and engineers are learning to apply their expertise more broadly. Professionals in the physical sciences find employment not only in the discipline of their degree but also in a wide variety of related careers where their analytic and reasoning abilities are valued.

For example, increasing numbers of physicists, mathematicians, and engineers find their skills valued in the financial arena. More than 14% of the firms recruiting at the Massachusetts Institute of Technology in 1995 were financial companies, nearly 3 times as many as in 1983. Graduates are being put to work writing software, using computers to capitalize on market inefficiencies, constructing financial models that predict fluctuations in securities prices, and designing complex mathematical tools to assess portfolio risk.

In engineering, careers are being transformed by several intersecting trends. International companies now draw employees from many nations, seeking out valued experts from a global pool of labor to work project by project. Companies value multilingual workers with a breadth of competencies—managerial as well as technical—and the ability to access and apply new scientific and technologic knowledge. The more flexible and mobile you can be, the more opportunities you will have and the greater will be your control over the shape of your career (IEEE video 1995; University of Texas at Dallas 1995).

The Case of the PhD

Although most people believe that PhDs work primarily as tenured research professors in academe, long-term trends show otherwise. Fewer than half are in tenure-track positions and almost half are in nonresearch positions.

For example, a graduate-student packet from the American Institute of Physics describes PhD physicists working in diverse positions: physical oceanographer, air-pollution expert, science education-consultant, computer-software de-

The Importance of Knowing Your Facts and Figures

As a scientist or engineer, you know the importance of not just making assumptions or listening to anecdotes when you're analyzing a situation in the laboratory or the field. The same is true when you are trying to understand graduate education or the job market.

For example, how many science and engineering PhDs do you think obtain employment in the academic employment market? 90%? 75%? The real answer, as shown in the graph on page 15 is less than 50% in 1991, and it is an illustration of a steadily declining trend. On the other hand, employment of science and engineering PhDs by business and industry is increasing in that same period. If you look at how many science and engineering PhDs are in tenure-track positions 5-8 years after receiving the PhD, you will find that it is less than one-third.

What is the employment marketplace like this year for those with bachelor's vs. master's vs. PhDs in different disciplines? How many people in different disciplines get master's vs. PhDs? How many years does it take to get a PhD in different disciplines? Is postdoctoral work in your discipline customary? How long does it usually take? What are the most common mechanisms being used for financial support of graduate students? There is no way of knowing the latest statistic in the ever-changing academic and employment market without taking some time to review the available information.

To find out information like this, make a stop at the National Research Council's *Career Planning Center For*

veloper, professor of history of physics, science journalist, partner in a venture-capital firm, astrophysicist, founder of a small corporation, staff scientist in an instrument firm, industrial ecologist, quantitative analyst with an international bank, educational-software consultant, developer of speech-recognition systems, and radiologic physicist (APS 1994).

Beginning Scientists and Engineers on the Internet (http://www2.nas.edu/cpc). One section of the center titled "Trends and Changes in the Job Market" analyzes such data from a student perspective. Another good source of information is your scientific or engineering disciplinary society. Many societies produce an annual employment guide that discusses the employment market for their discipline—especially for recent graduates. In addition, the National Science Foundation issues each year a report titled *Science and Engineering Indicators* that also discusses these statistics.

So take the time to look at the available facts and figures about the job market and graduate education before taking that next big step.

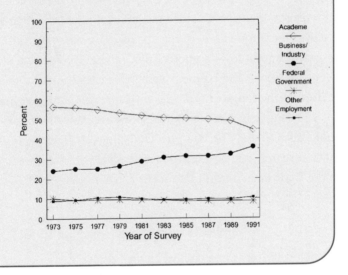

Similarly, PhD chemists have success in moving beyond the laboratory bench to a wide range of careers. Within companies, they might move into marketing, production, manufacturing, sales, or management. Or they can move into such related fields as environmental chemistry, public policy, education, journalism, scientific translation, law, banking, medicine, patent law, public service, and regulation. PhD biologists might move to those and other careers, such as biotechnology, pharmaceuticals, biochemical processing, ecology-policy analysis, and patent law.

Engineers, of course, have long moved transparently between academe, industry, and business. All scientists and engineers potentially have the opportunity to use non-research skills within science- and engineering-oriented organizations by managing other scientists, developing budgets, and producing plans for new R&D activities (Kirschner 1995).

Such examples reflect a fundamental shift in the conduct of research. Increasingly, the most interesting work is being done at the interfaces between chemistry, biology, physics, engineering, geology, and other disciplines. That has the effect of blurring the boundaries between traditional disciplines, so the range of activities in science and engineering is beginning to look more like a continuum than a set of discrete disciplines. The complex challenges of interdisciplinary research demand a broader preparation than does a more traditional disciplinary focus (Tobias et al. 1995).

Evaluating Possible Careers

Even if your career might change direction as you advance, your first steps are important ones. How do you know where to begin?

Do not ignore what is right under your nose: your own faculty adviser and, if you are a graduate student, your research or laboratory group. By watching the people around you, you can learn a great deal about the roles that a faculty member plays. Your adviser could be, at various times, a teacher, a business manager, a mentor, an author, a committee member, a boss. Which of those roles is appealing to you?

If you are an undergraduate or beginning graduate student, you are probably not ready to choose a career. But you can start asking questions and watching people in their work. If you learn early what your options can be, you will be ready to ask the right questions when your time comes to find a position.

Evaluating jobs also means dealing with attitudes. Some faculty members and students assign a lower status to non-research jobs for people who have PhDs. As a result, PhD students who plan for such jobs might be told that they are wasting their education or letting their advisers down. That attitude is less prevalent in some professions, notably engineering and some biology-related fields, where nonacademic employment is the norm. Also, negative attitudes toward nonacademic employment are often less evident during times of job scarcity. But if you do encounter such an attitude remember that a wide variety of positions can be as challenging and gratifying for PhD scientists and engineers as traditional research positions. Back up your assertion with facts and figures, including the profiles presented in this guide and facts about the employment situation from the Academy's Internet career-planning center.

Tempo and Environment

Consider the tempo and environment of various careers. Are you attracted to the pursuit of knowledge, the search for something new, the freedom to follow your curiosity? If so, you might be best suited for a career as a basic researcher, even if it means spending long hours in the laboratory or library. Or do you work best with other people and perhaps dream of the excitement of running a large operation, making executive decisions, and bringing new scientific ideas to the marketplace? Many basic researchers eventually do those things—if they have strong team and leadership skills.

Think about the day-by-day activities of a career. Will they provide challenges that stimulate you? Do you like the depth of a single project or the variety of a changing scene? Do you prefer a more-formal or a less-formal atmosphere? How will your work mesh with family life and other obligations? How much will a job pay—not just when you start, but as you advance?

For example, PhD physicists who work in industry were asked, What aspects of your work are rewarding? First on their list was the challenge of solving interesting and complex problems. Second was the satisfaction of working with people. Third was seeing a project yield a successful and useful product. Last on the list was basic research. If that order of priorities appeals to you, you might be suited to a career in industry (AIP 1994).

Relating Your Education to Your Occupation

It is possible that you will begin as a laboratory scientist or engineer and move on to a management or other leadership position. If you recognize such possibilities, you can design your graduate education so that you are equipped for many kinds of nonresearch activities.

Remember, also, that even graduate-level scientists and engineers in "traditional" academic careers need a broad range of skills. The most successful of them might spend 70-80 hours a week at their jobs, a large proportion of which is spent in writing, lecturing, and discussing matters far removed from research.

How does a CHEMICAL ENGINEER . . .

Get to be a BUILDING DESIGNER?

It might seem strange to some people that Steve M. Hays, who was trained at Vanderbilt University as a chemical engineer, is now a partner in an architectural firm. But it is not strange to Mr. Hays.

"When I moved from a position at DuPont as a process engineer," he recalls, "it appeared that I was leaving the chemical engineering profession. This hasn't happened. We've entered an age of increasingly sophisticated building construction. Understanding the chemical composition of materials is critically important, so my training is very appropriate for this career."

At Gobbell Hays Partners, Inc., in Nashville, TN, he is active in the design of "safe" buildings and in providing comprehensive industrial hygiene and safety services for facilities with health, safety, or environmental problems. One specialty is devising safe management practices for dealing with health hazards, such as asbestos, lead, and radon. He has consulted on the development of guidance manuals by the National Institute of Building Sciences and worked with the Environmental Protection Agency to write asbestos regulations for the nation's schools.

continued

A big step in changing careers, Mr. Hays admits, was simply "summoning up the courage to make the switch." Once he did, the transition went smoothly, for several reasons. One was that he and his architect partner, Ron Gobbell, were willing and able to exchange expertise. Equally important was Mr. Hays' conviction that he had something to offer.

"A chemical engineer in the building industry doesn't seem so far-fetched when you consider that the chemical engineering curriculum provides a base in all the engineering disciplines. I can meet with consulting engineers of other disciplines on an equal footing when discussing building projects. A positive approach turns out to be essential—an attitude of 'I have things to contribute here.' It's been my experience that professionals in building design are very receptive to the expertise of a chemical engineer."

Personal Values and Your Occupation

Think about possible careers from many angles: Is the atmosphere intellectually challenging enough for you? Do you hope to teach a lot or a little? Are you more comfortable in a campus environment or in the world of business (Kennedy 1995)? How important is the prestige of your position? Are you planning to do what your parents always wanted you to do or what you want to do?

Think as deeply as you can about your personal values. Do you have a need to help others or to protect the environment? Will you be doing those things in your work? Visit as many workplaces as you can to gain valuable clues about settings where you believe that you would be comfortable.

Consider also your present family situation. If you are married, do you expect your spouse to move to a new location? Do you have or plan to have children? Can you support them? If you have had to borrow money, how much debt will you carry beyond your school years?

Evaluating an Occupation

To make such evaluations, you need to learn the characteristics of different occupations. Talk with faculty, friends, or acquaintances who have jobs that appeal to you; accompany them to work and ask about their careers. Even people who do not know you personally are often willing to tell you about their jobs. "Shadowing" someone for even a single workday can give you the flavor of a job and its routines. Do this early—as an undergraduate, if possible—before you get too busy to take time from your work. Such information-gathering can build networks that serve you well in the future.

Evaluating Yourself

Frank is happy majoring in chemistry, but when friends ask him what kind of career he is planning, he has no answer. He is not even sure whether he fits in academe, in industry, or in government.

► What should Frank be doing to find his direction?

See Appendix A for a discussion of this scenario.

Pursue every opportunity (during a summer, for example) to gain practical experience. Seek out cooperative education programs, which are explicitly designed for this purpose. Try to experience first-hand the conditions of the working environment that you contemplate. You might learn a lot about yourself and about different careers by doing volunteer work in a hospital, classroom, or laboratory. Internships can reveal the feeling or atmosphere of a particular discipline and introduce you to the kinds of people who work in that field.

You might think that you know exactly what you want to do, or you might have already begun to work. Even so, it pays to investigate adjacent areas in case opportunities in your chosen field are limited or the field has matured beyond its phase of rapid growth (Peters 1992). For example, suppose that microbiology is your choice, but you seem to be stalled at the postdoctoral level. A degree in microbiology might allow you to find gratifying work in a biotechnology firm. Suppose that you studied electrical engineering to work in the space program, but jobs are scarce; a double degree with environmental engineering might give you

How does a MATHEMATICS MAJOR . . .

Get to be an ACTUARY?

Russell Greig excelled in mathematics as an undergraduate at Florida A&M University. His goals were to use mathematics in a practical way, to work in the "real world," and to earn a good income. He was planning a career in civil engineering when his calculus professor took him aside.

"He said, 'You're doing well enough in math; have you considered actuarial science?' I hadn't, so I checked it out in the *Jobs Almanac*, which said it was a growing field. After some reluctance—I was already pretty far along in engineering—I decided to give it a try."

Now, just 5 years later, Mr. Greig is one examination away from being a fellow of the Casualty Actuarial Society, the rough equivalent of a PhD in actuarial mathematics. He gained a head start by taking the first two actuarial examinations as an undergraduate; 10 are required for fellowship status. As a result, he was offered a job on graduation by the National Council on Compensation Insurance, in Boca Raton, Florida, an insurance advisory company. His first assignment was to produce a new set of summary exhibits derived from detailed claim data needed by insurance companies, actuaries, and legislatures. He is now calculating reserves for the workers' compensation "residual" insurance

continued

market. At the same time, he is approaching the end of his studies.

"Since I graduated, I've been spending close to 400 hours every 4 months studying for the exams," he says. "The company gives me 120 hours, the rest I do at night and on weekends. The competition is pretty steep, so you have to do well. If you do, job prospects are excellent and you gain high respect in the profession. At the fellowship level you're at the top and you can pretty much decide where you want to work. I'll probably stay in the South; I'm from the Virgin Islands and I can't take the cold."

Mr. Greig encourages students who enjoy applied mathematics to look into the field. "I recommend it to those who enjoy number-crunching, who want to see immediate, practical results from what they're doing. You have to be prepared to pay your dues, but there's plenty of opportunity. There are only about 2,500 casualty actuaries in the world, and the field is still growing.

"Math majors have other good choices in applied fields. One is the financial area, where there is demand for people who can quantify financial risk models and also can present what they're doing clearly to others who are not sophisticated in math. In fact, when I'm done with these exams I'm going to take the Chartered Financial Analyst exams, which are like a shortcut to an MBA in finance. This allows you to do more asset-related work.

"Another growth area is computer science and programming. I often work with programmers who don't understand the math involved. If you know the math to begin with, you'll be able to write your own ticket. The math is where it begins."

more options. For ideas, check university placement offices, professional employment companies, professional societies, and the want ads in major newspapers and journals, which can tell you which fields are searching for people. Use referrals from faculty, students, and your disciplinary society to find and talk with people in fields that might be new to you.

Many scientists and engineers flourish as self-employed consultants. Independent, self-reliant people might find diverse possibilities in doing contract work for businesses, industries, or government agencies. But people who have taken such steps caution against taking them prematurely. To raise your chances of success, develop your contacts, try working in a field that you have already mastered, and be sure that you have the financial resources to get through periods of low income. Part-time self-employment can be a source of income—and contacts—while you are looking for a position.

If after considerable investigation you still do not see your career on the horizon, do not assume that it doesn't exist. If you know what you like to do and become good at it, your interest might evolve naturally into a job that is an extension of your own special interests and activities. One of the benefits of an innovative, fast-changing society like ours is that people are able and even encouraged to create their own niches.

Evaluating Your Own Strengths and Weaknesses

While you are evaluating possible careers, take a close look at yourself as a person. Are you innovative or conventional? Timid or bold? Do you thrive on constant challenge? How important is your career, compared with family and other activities? Some positions in science and engineering involve long hours and a high degree of dedication.

For a fulfilling career, there must be a good match between your natural abilities and what is expected in various professional positions. A useful exercise is to ask yourself what you have enjoyed most in your life and where you think that you have been most useful. Then ask what you have enjoyed least or have found most frustrating. Compare the two lists. Why did you enjoy or dislike each activity? Do you think that your attitude would change if you had more education or training? Would it make a difference if you did it in a different setting or with different people? By examining apparent mismatches, you can learn to evaluate your own strengths and weaknesses in the context of possible jobs.

Take advantage of computer aids and self-assessments; talk to students, teachers, friends outside school, and a guidance counselor. Planning and placement offices provide testing and counseling for students and alumni. Such tests as the Myers-Briggs Type Indicator (a personality inventory) and the Strong Interest Inventory (which compares a person's interests with those of people employed in particular occupations) might help in finding the career best suited to your temperament.

Because it is difficult to see yourself objectively, seek out other people who might have a different picture of you. A friend or colleague might see strengths invisible to you or advise you against a career that seems wrong for you. An undergraduate adviser can be especially useful—especially if he or she knows you personally as well as academically.

Many publications offer inexpensive, do-it-yourself ways to assess your skills. Check your library, bookstore, and career center for guides that help you take inventory of your skills and preferences and match the results with the characteristics of different fields. The most popular is *What Color Is Your Parachute?*, by Richard Bolles, a new revision of which appears each November. Bolles studied chemical engineering at the Massachusetts Institute of Technology and earned a degree in physics from Harvard. He offers many aids to help you to determine which skills you most enjoy using, the context in which you want to use them, and careers in which you can apply them (Jensen 1995). Other tools are now available online and can be reached via the National Research Council (NRC) *Career Planning Center For Beginning Scientists and Engineers* (http://www2.nas.edu/cpc).

Assessment of your skills, of your preferences, and of the careers that might be available to you continues as you complete each degree and gain work experience. The time to begin is now, and you should renew this assessment annually throughout your career.

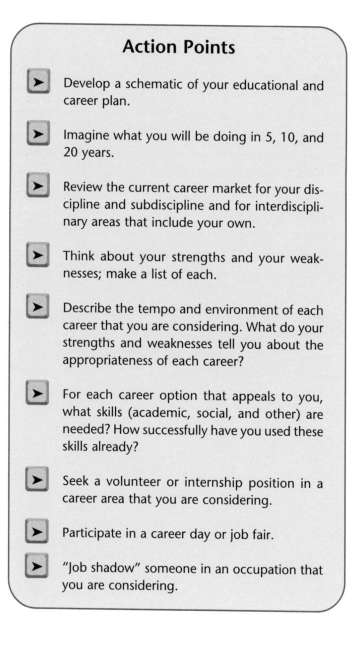

Action Points

➤ Develop a schematic of your educational and career plan.

➤ Imagine what you will be doing in 5, 10, and 20 years.

➤ Review the current career market for your discipline and subdiscipline and for interdisciplinary areas that include your own.

➤ Think about your strengths and your weaknesses; make a list of each.

➤ Describe the tempo and environment of each career that you are considering. What do your strengths and weaknesses tell you about the appropriateness of each career?

➤ For each career option that appeals to you, what skills (academic, social, and other) are needed? How successfully have you used these skills already?

➤ Seek a volunteer or internship position in a career area that you are considering.

➤ Participate in a career day or job fair.

➤ "Job shadow" someone in an occupation that you are considering.

3

WHAT SURVIVAL SKILLS AND PERSONAL ATTRIBUTES DO YOU NEED TO SUCCEED?

In the last chapter, we discussed matching your personality and natural abilities with the kind of performance required in various careers. Some of those skills are technical, such as the ability to operate or design complex equipment. Others allow you to apply your technical skills: the ability to reason, to spot interesting problems, to formulate hypotheses, to test those hypotheses. These allied skills acquired in graduate school are more powerful than many students recognize and can be applied to many other kinds of jobs and careers.

What Are Skills and Attributes?

A potential employer will assume that as a scientist or engineer, you have advanced technical skills. But some of them, including the analytic and problem-solving abilities that are central to what you do as a researcher, might remain invisible unless you are able to display them. That is, unless you also have such survival skills as communication, teaching, mentoring, teamwork, and leadership, your total effectiveness might be difficult to see.

Basic among survival skills are social skills, which are increasingly important in all kinds of jobs, including research positions. They are used when you participate in a seminar, lead a team effort to solve a research problem, or give a public presentation. They should not be considered optional or extra. Scientists and engineers doing research are working more and more directly with nonscientists, members of the public, and clients to solve problems. All technical abilities being equal, the candidate who has strong social skills will be hired.

In many jobs, you will spend a large part of your time in practicing nontechnical skills. In 1994, the American Institute of Physics asked several thousand PhD physicists working in industry, government, and academe which skills they used most frequently in their jobs. The skills that they ranked highest were problem-solving, interpersonal skills, and technical writing. All those apply to fields throughout science and engineering and can be sharpened, as suggested in this chapter.

Skills are developed as we mature, and your years in school are a good time to make sure that you have the ones you need. Students who emerge as young scientists with a deficit of social and communication skills might be severely handicapped in pursuing a satisfying career. As the range of employment for scientists and engineers expands, especially in the nonacademic world, it is vital to gain as many skills as possible before leaving the university setting.

Attributes are aspects of your nature (although they can be developed). Unlike skills, which enable you to *do* something, attributes enable you to *be* someone. Sometimes they

How does a CHEMISTRY MAJOR . . .
Get to be a PROFESSOR?

Janice Hicks's father, who worked for a pharmaceutical company, was a major influence on her choice of career. She paid attention as he described the excitement of chemistry and his reverence for scientific research. By the time she was a first-year student at Bryn Mawr College, she knew that she wanted to be an academic researcher.

Today, Dr. Hicks is a tenured professor and respected researcher at Georgetown University—recipient of a Presidential Young Investigator Award. She has pioneered the use of ultrafast lasers to study surface phenomena relevant to atmospheric chemistry and biophysical chemistry. A long-term goal is to understand the three-dimensional shape of proteins absorbed at interfaces, such as the cell membrane.

"Graduate school was a natural step for me," Dr. Hicks recalls. "From my father I'd absorbed the belief that research was the 'ultimate' occupation. When I got to college I felt confident about my love for chemistry, I received excellent preparation, and the professors were people I wanted to be like. I remember how impressed I was when I saw my first academic procession—I thought that was the right place to be."

After graduating as a chemistry major, she took a year off from school and learned two important lessons. A sum-

continued

mer in an industrial laboratory taught her that she did not want to work in industry. And a stint in a biophysics laboratory at the University of Pennsylvania taught her that she preferred the precision and molecular scale of physical chemistry to larger-scale biologic work.

When the time came to choose a graduate school, she was not particularly methodical. She selected Columbia University because she had enjoyed a visit to a friend at Barnard and because she wanted to live in New York. But it turned out to be a good match; she verified her passion for chemistry and built expertise in using ultrafast lasers to study chemical processes in liquids. And whenever the laser broke down, she and her friends could take the subway downtown to the Metropolitan Opera.

But it was not until she went back to Penn for post-doctoral work that she really knew that she could be a professor. "I had heard you have to be the best to go into academe, and I was still questioning my ability. Then I had a mentor who changed all that. He gave me the push I needed, and once it came, my confidence grew.

"This is an issue for many women, in particular. Women don't apply for academe positions in the proportion to the number graduating, and I think confidence is the issue. They tend to hold back, to wait for a signal from mentors. Many mentors don't think to give this signal, without realizing how important it is.

"A lot of young women have heard that you've got to be the best to go into academe, and when you do, you have to go to a top-10 university. If they only realized how many hundreds of universities there are out there that need good professors!"

Her desire to help students with such issues is an important feature of her life at Georgetown, where about 50% of her time is spent in teaching. "I went to a small college where undergraduates got a lot of attention. I wanted to be at a place where the undergrads are very good, which they are here, and where I could give some of that attention back."

Her advice to students applying to graduate school: "Be very good writers and speakers. That's key to getting a job and getting grants. And as you begin, get a good mentor, or preferably more than one, who are younger profs who have just gone through this process. There's a lot of 'oral tradition' about getting through graduate school—things that you need to know but won't find written down."

Two issues that present challenges to new assistant professors are tenure and research funding. "The tenure process at Georgetown was not too bad," said Hicks. The initial job interviews are conducted with much rigor, and the faculty claims to 'make the tenure decision,' at that point. There are no quotas here for number of publications or grants." In the area of research funding, the federal, academic and industrial sources are undergoing a major shift. "Everyone is having trouble getting grants, not just new faculty. Promotion decision will have to take today's funding climate into account."

are inherent; at other times these attributes are learned from the example of parents, friends, teachers, and other mentors, as well as through personal experience.

For example, how well do you interact with others? Do you accept responsibility for your failures or do you blame them on someone else? Are you enthusiastic, alert, thorough, imaginative, self-reliant?

A crucial attribute is the ability to perform your work ethically. Because this ability does not appear to be a "skill" in the sense of communication or teamwork, for example, it might be easy to neglect. However, responsible conduct is an underpinning of any successful career. Another student guide from COSEPUP, *On Being a Scientist: Responsible Conduct in Research*, discusses ethical issues. Although written for researchers, it addresses many issues, such as sharing credit for work performed, that apply in any field. In all activities, it is important to keep in mind that scientists and engineers have the same human frailties as other people.

If you choose experimental science, check your degree of perseverance. It is in the nature of research that most experiments fail and many ideas turn out to be wrong . Scientific knowledge progresses in fits and starts and is marked by gradual community acceptance of results that stand up over time.

Attributes change over time; you can allow them to languish or you can develop them through practice and attention. Have frank discussions with friends, teachers, mentors, and colleagues. Through effort and practice, you can learn to be more attentive, flexible, or decisive.

The purpose of understanding and working on your attributes—as well as your skills—is to make your working life more successful and rewarding. Although you can sharpen your skills and strengthen your attributes through-out your career, graduate school might constitute the last opportunity to take advantage of the courses, tutors, and informal learning environment found in institutions of higher learning.

Appendix B provides a list of skills and attributes. Rank-ing yourself from 1 to 5 for each skill and attribute is a worth-while exercise to do before you read the remainder of this chapter.

Communication Skills

Scientists and engineers in all positions have to be able to communicate the purpose and relevance of their work, both orally and in writing. If you are a teacher, you must communicate with your students. If you work in industry, you must communicate with managers and co-workers (many of whom will not be scientists or engineers) and per-haps with customers. If you are responsible for raising funds for your research, you must market your ideas effectively, write proposals, and generate enthusiasm for your research. If you work in public policy or government, you might have to communicate with the press and other members of the public.

Good communication skills are often needed to get a good job in the first place. If you are clear in expressing your thoughts and articulating your accomplishments and at-tributes, an interviewer is more likely to form a favorable impression of you and gain an understanding of your skills.

If you are a student, a forthright and outgoing commu-nication style can help to build a better relationship with your adviser. If you can describe your work and your goals

Communication Skills

As she begins graduate school in electrical engineering, Lee decides to attend a career-counseling session on campus. She is fairly sure that she will end up working for industry, so she wants to improve her communication skills and knowledge of corporate culture. But her curriculum is already full, and she is reluctant to add extra courses.

> How can Lee build skills without adding to her course load?

See Appendix A for a discussion of this scenario.

clearly, you are likely to get better advice in return. When it comes time for you to be a mentor to younger students, the value of your guidance will depend on your ability to express yourself.

You need to communicate with colleagues to keep up with trends, to collaborate on projects, and to find a new position. This kind of communication requires clarity of expression, ability to organize thoughts, ability to be a good listener, and empathy for the lives and interests of others. Those skills might not come easy to one who is shy or prefers to work alone. But with practice and the help of friends, they can be improved.

In many environments, particularly as your career advances, you will want to explain your work to nonscientists or scientists trained in other fields who make decisions about funding, facilities, or distribution of capital (human and financial). You should practice by describing your work in simple terms to friends and family at every opportunity.

Give special attention to your writing ability. As an undergraduate, you might do a senior project; as a master's student, you will probably write a thesis; as a doctoral student, you will write a dissertation. As a graduate student, you will also be expected to write papers for publication in journals. All these writing projects must be done to high standards and become evidence of your ability when the time comes to seek employment.

If you think that you need help, take a class in scientific writing or ask a journalism professor to arrange a seminar on the topic. Solicit and learn from responses to papers and proposals when you write them. Take a speech class, join a Toastmaster's Club,[1] or volunteer to talk about your specialty to a local civic group or high school class. Graduate students should form a cooperative group in which students make presentations to each other and agree to provide (and accept) honest responses. Communicate with others via Internet, trying to express your ideas clearly.

If English is not your native language, you must develop English-language skills. Writing exercises will pay off when it comes time to write a thesis, job application, study plan, or grant proposal; speaking exercises will help you to ask questions, communicate with professors, and participate in interviews. It is comforting to spend time with compatriots, but it is easiest to learn the local language (and culture) by mingling with those who speak English. Good language skills will make it easier to find employment, to teach, and to learn from your professors.

---

[1]Toastmasters is an international organization of people from many fields who are attempting to improve their public speaking ability. Local chapters are common throughout the United States.

Teaching Skills

Teaching skills are important for finding a job in academe and elsewhere. You might find yourself doing considerable teaching, in its broader sense, in business and industry, as well as in the classroom.

For example, if you want an entrepreneur or venture-capital company to support your work in a new technical field, you will have to communicate the special potential of your project. An investor in a biotechnology company will need to understand what biotechnology is and how it works. Or, you might be called on to explain technical subjects to members of a marketing or sales department.

Teaching as you remember being taught in school might not lead to success. Increasingly, the successful teacher is a coach more than a lecturer and is able to use different styles for students with different learning patterns. Most campuses have courses or centers to improve teaching. Centers often provide guidance to teaching assistants and are developing teaching methods that are more "student-friendly" for diverse populations.

You can experiment with improvement techniques on your own. Have one of your classes videotaped—always an eye-opening experience. Become familiar with one of the guides to college teaching; *Teaching Tips*, by Wilbert McKeachie and others, now in its ninth edition, is comprehensive and useful. Pick up new ideas from journals and lectures by renowned educators. Attend presentations and pay attention to both content and teaching techniques, good and bad. Seek out opportunities to practice what you learn in a variety of settings. Ask for responses from peers and from your audience.

How does a PHYSICIST . . .

Get to be a FINANCIAL RESEARCHER?

Mark Ferrari was in graduate school, doing research at Berkeley on magnetic structures in superconductors, when he began to doubt his passion for experimental physics. His suspicion was confirmed after he was hired by Bell Labs, where he found physics to be "a pretty lonely enterprise."

"I was basically working alone in a room with a machine," he recalls. "That didn't suit my temperament. Also, I was not getting a sense that the problems I was working on were making a difference to anyone."

He moved to BARRA, Inc., a global investment technology firm in Berkeley, and found that his research activities supplied what was missing. "Here I'm reminded every day that what I do makes a difference. BARRA builds risk assessment and trading tools, and my research group develops the next generation of models. It's truly satisfying to give a presentation about your work and have clients call to find out how quickly they'll be able to get their hands on it."

Dr. Ferrari emphasizes that his route is not for everyone. "I wouldn't say to a student, get a degree in physics because it's good preparation for a career in finance. The reason to study physics is that you love physics. What I would say is that you should keep your options open, cast your net

continued

widely, figure out what the possibilities are. If you like study-ing science and think it will be your career, that's great; you should do it. But don't treat grad school as a trade school. When you're interested in a subject, take a course in it, even if you have to fight with your adviser to do it. Talk with people who work in that field. What you can do with your education is limited only when you don't know what's out there."

Mentoring Skills

Mentoring is related to teaching and is just as amenable to improvement. If teaching is primarily the imparting of facts, mentoring is imparting procedures: ways of thinking, doing research, and approaching new problems. The best faculty advisers are mentors. They teach not only by instruction and participation, but also by example and they have an interest not only in your performance, but also in your progress as a person. A good mentor relationship is personal: a mentor should have opportunities to discuss issues of ethical, ideologic, and philosophic concern, as well as more practical matters.

There are many ways to begin developing your mentoring skills even as an undergraduate. Take advantage of informal opportunities to advise others in the laboratory setting. If your university does not offer training in formal advising, try to start new programs via student associations or other means. Organize panel discussions on advising. Volunteer to advise or tutor high-school students or undergraduates; sometimes, student advisers are paid for their work. If you would like to break in gradually, try collective mentoring, as when a group of older students in a laboratory help to acclimate a group of newcomers. The more you learn about mentoring others, the more you can understand what you can learn from your own advisers, and they from you.

Such experience prepares you for a role in business and industry, where you might be a mentor and teacher of younger workers and fellow staff members. It also prepares you to become a manager; managers often act as mentors for junior colleagues.

Your efforts to sharpen your mentoring skills can be rewarded many times over as you move into your career. Few pleasures are greater than that of inspiring and guiding enthusiastic younger scientists and engineers as they prepare to launch their own careers.

Team Skills

Research has become a more collective enterprise in academe, government, and industry than in the past. One result of that trend is that graduate students in science and engineering are more likely to work as members of a research team. This can already be seen in the ever-increasing number of multiple-author papers in the scholarly literature.

Beyond the conduct of research, however, you will need good team skills because science and engineering are becoming more integrated into other activities. In any career, you are likely to find yourself working with managers, administrators, committee members, and planners. If you work in a college or university, you might serve on various committees, many of which are composed of nonscientists and nonacademic people. If you work in industry, you might serve on a team that includes people in management, marketing, accounting, and sales.

There are many ways to strengthen team skills. Practice brainstorming with other students, enjoying the synergy of multiple minds. Take part in active team learning exercises in a classroom setting, where the group extends the knowledge of all participants through sharing and mutual interest. Join disciplinary societies, campus-based gatherings, regional or national conferences, and discussions on the Internet to meet new people and exchange information. You

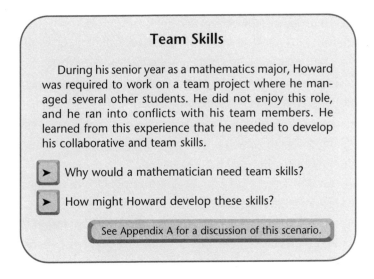

Team Skills

During his senior year as a mathematics major, Howard was required to work on a team project where he managed several other students. He did not enjoy this role, and he ran into conflicts with his team members. He learned from this experience that he needed to develop his collaborative and team skills.

➤ Why would a mathematician need team skills?

➤ How might Howard develop these skills?

See Appendix A for a discussion of this scenario.

also can help to set up activities like career days or resume workshops, which often arise from the initiative of students. Each of these steps can strengthen team skills, increase the size of your network, and prepare you to function more effectively in your professional career.

None of this is said to diminish the importance of individual scholarship. Learn what you can from others—but there must also be times to be alone, to ponder, to find out what you think and who you are.

Leadership Skills

Leadership is a quality that must be communicated to others, through both actions and words. There are many opportunities early in your career to develop this quality and to observe it in others. Volunteer to organize a group discussion or project; help a group of undergraduates to learn about research and be responsible in planning meetings with your committee and in reminding members to attend.

Look around you for role models and mentors. A leader in science and engineering might take on various responsibilities: supervising a laboratory, heading a research team, managing a department, or planning new projects. Who among the people you know does a good job as a leader, and what qualities make this possible?

Leadership is a rare quality because it has two facets: a leader must know the goal of an activity and must be able to organize and motivate others to reach the goal. That requires some understanding of the skills and personality of everyone in the group. To develop your capacity for empathy, talk with others about their projects and challenges.

The most-effective leaders are not dictators. Exercise leadership by doing or illustrating rather than by ordering. Others will be more willing to follow a leader who is a servant first; your own activity as an honest, conscientious, and helpful teammate will inspire the same activity in others.

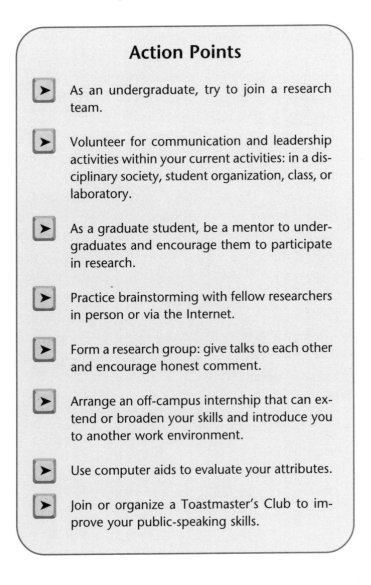

Action Points

➤ As an undergraduate, try to join a research team.

➤ Volunteer for communication and leadership activities within your current activities: in a disciplinary society, student organization, class, or laboratory.

➤ As a graduate student, be a mentor to undergraduates and encourage them to participate in research.

➤ Practice brainstorming with fellow researchers in person or via the Internet.

➤ Form a research group: give talks to each other and encourage honest comment.

➤ Arrange an off-campus internship that can extend or broaden your skills and introduce you to another work environment.

➤ Use computer aids to evaluate your attributes.

➤ Join or organize a Toastmaster's Club to improve your public-speaking skills.

WHAT EDUCATION DO YOU NEED TO REACH YOUR CAREER GOALS?

As mentioned in the preface, this chapter discusses a wide range of educational questions, beginning with those of interest primarily to undergraduates and ending with the transition to full-time employment. For quick reading, you can use the headings to pick out particular topics. However, we feel that most of the themes discussed in this chapter will be of interest to students at all levels, as well as to faculty advisers and administrators.

The Undergraduate Years

Many students start thinking about the possibility of a career when their interest is ignited by a high-school or undergraduate teacher or some other role model. This is the time to start meeting and talking with scientists and engineers in fields that interest you. These early contacts can be crucial in helping you to navigate the terrain of science and engineering as you move through your career.

The undergraduate years are probably your best chance

to take a broad variety of classes outside your primary discipline that might be useful later. For example, a mathematics major who takes accounting is better equipped to do actuarial work. An ecology major would gain perspective from classes in environmental engineering or environmental policy that can have lifelong benefits.

Classes in economics, sociology, history, philosophy, English (with emphasis on composition), foreign language, and psychology, spread through the undergraduate years, are immensely useful in helping you to acquire understanding, different experiences, and maturity. As science and technology become more central in our society, scientists and engineers become more involved with other, nonresearch domains of human experience.

An effective way for students to learn about graduate education is to join (or form) a study group to discuss homework and share concerns. In a university setting, you can meet with graduate students and postdoctoral researchers and gain insights about specific graduate programs, possible careers, and the current job market. You can join student chapters of scientific and engineering disciplinary societies, both general (such as the Society of Women Engineers) and specific (such as the American Chemical Society). These can help you gain leadership and communication skills and can often assist in networking with senior members who can provide advice and possibly employment opportunities once you graduate.

Work with your undergraduate adviser not only to plan the science or engineering courses you will need, but also to ensure a well-rounded experience in this, your last general educational experience. Ask your adviser to provide guidance in thinking about what knowledge you will need as you move through your studies and into your career.

Remember that you are partly responsible for building a helpful relationship with your undergraduate adviser. Prepare for meetings with your adviser by thinking about where your interests and talents lie; think of four or five points you will make. The more you take the initiative and pose carefully thought-out questions, the more likely it is that your adviser, a busy faculty or staff member with a heavy workload, will take the time and effort necessary to be an effective mentor. He or she cannot divine your concerns; you must express them.

If you are considering graduate school, take the Graduate Record Examination (GRE) during your junior or senior year. This is a test required for admission to most graduate schools. Discuss with your adviser your potential for advanced study. The results of the GRE, your grade point average, and your adviser's opinion will help you to decide whether you have the potential for graduate school.

Decisions About Graduate School

As an undergraduate, you might find it hard to get a clear picture of the graduate environment. This is where an effective faculty adviser, as someone who has "been there," can provide invaluable help. Seek out your adviser (or another mentor) and learn what you can as early as possible.

Deciding Whether to Attend Graduate School

You do not necessarily need a graduate degree to have a career in science or engineering. For example, engineers with a bachelor's degree can often move upward quickly in

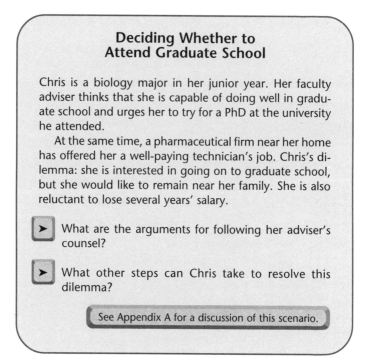

**Deciding Whether to
Attend Graduate School**

Chris is a biology major in her junior year. Her faculty adviser thinks that she is capable of doing well in graduate school and urges her to try for a PhD at the university he attended.

At the same time, a pharmaceutical firm near her home has offered her a well-paying technician's job. Chris's dilemma: she is interested in going on to graduate school, but she would like to remain near her family. She is also reluctant to lose several years' salary.

➤ What are the arguments for following her adviser's counsel?

➤ What other steps can Chris take to resolve this dilemma?

See Appendix A for a discussion of this scenario.

their profession and, with luck and hard work, can even break into top management. However, if your goal is to direct research or to teach at the college or university level, you will probably want a PhD (Bailey and Leavitt 1982). In undergraduate school, you learn what is already known; in a master's program, you build your knowledge to a higher technical level; in a doctoral program, you learn to add to the body of scientific and technical knowledge.

At all levels, graduate education is both rigorous and focused. It is not simply a bigger and more-advanced version of undergraduate schooling, where you meet a wide range of subjects and acquire general skills. As a graduate student, you pursue at much greater depth knowledge that

How does an ELECTRONICS ENGINEER . . .

Get to be a SCIENCE JOURNALIST?

Four years ago, Shankar Vedantam had mapped out a career in management. He was about to take his final examinations in electronic engineering at Bangalore University, in India, and then enter an MBA program. But at that moment the country's prime minister was assassinated, his examinations were postponed, and he was prevented from entering the management school for another year.

To pass the time, he accepted a job as a newspaper reporter with *The Times of India*—a decision that changed his life. He was quickly hooked on the realism of his new job, and he relished the responsibility of helping people to understand current events. A year later, he earned a master's in journalism at Stanford University and soon moved to a big-city job at the *Philadelphia Inquirer*. He is now a medicine-science reporter for Knight-Ridder's Washington bureau.

"There is pleasure in straddling two fields," he says, "of bringing information from one area to another. I moved into science journalism because it seemed like a very neat way to capitalize on knowledge that I already had. In modern culture there is a huge knowledge base, but we haven't spread

continued

that knowledge very well. I feel that spreading it may be as important as generating it or acquiring it.

"It's hard to find good jobs in journalism. As with science and research, the market is competitive and may even be shrinking. Still, there will always be a demand for people who have technical skills and who can write about science clearly. Many people feel intimidated by science; they will always welcome someone who can explain it to them.

"My training in engineering is an excellent background for science writing. By that I don't mean so much the specific information I learned in school; that's changing all the time. What counts more is familiarity with the language of science. People who are not familiar with that language tend to pull away from something they don't understand. When I find something I don't understand, I just go out there and ask some questions. The same pattern of questions and answers tends to repeat, whether the subject is computers or medicine.

Mr. Vedantam advises that the best way to get into science writing is "just to do it. Write stories for a university newspaper, take a course in writing. Like most skills, it's learned by practice. Even if you don't become a science writer, you'll always benefit from having stronger writing skills."

is concentrated in a single field. It requires a love of your subject and a new depth of commitment.

Obtaining an advanced degree, especially a PhD, entails sacrifice. It requires delaying your entry, by many years, into a "real" job. Starting a family might also be difficult, and graduate students will probably be unable to buy a house or perhaps even a car. You might at times envy colleagues who went straight from a bachelor's degree into the job market and are already well advanced in their careers. Your love for your subject might be your best guide in deciding whether to go on to graduate school.

There is no simple formula to use to decide whether you should attend graduate school; your love for your subject may be your best guide. For a discussion of more of the issues involved, see the scenario "Deciding Whether to Attend Graduate School," and the related discussion in Appendix A.

In general, if you are excited by studying, problem-solving, discovering new facts, and exploring new ideas, you are likely to find graduate school a rewarding experience. Or you might have more practical goals: to enhance your job satisfaction, level of responsibility, earning power, and freedom to make your own decisions (CGS 1989). If you feel at home in mathematics and science and want to dig deeper, graduate experience can provide a powerful introduction to a professional life in science or engineering.

Deciding When to Attend Graduate School

Some students choose to work full-time for a while after receiving a bachelor's or master's degree and then return to school. That might be a good strategy if you are "burned out" by courses and examinations and need a break from school. You might also learn a great deal and see your field from a new perspective.

In some fields, such as engineering, it is common to begin work immediately after college. Later, students might take graduate courses while working; many employers financially support continuing education. That approach can increase your skills and job opportunities and allow you to work at the same time.

Moving directly into employment might not suit everyone. But it can be difficult to give up a full salary later to return to school, and it can be a struggle to regain the momentum and intensity of full-time study. Similarly, attending school part-time or at night does not provide the same intense learning experience as joining a group of your peers for concentrated, full-time work in an academic setting (Bailey and Leavitt 1982).

Some students might consider part-time graduate study because of family or financial obligations. But graduate work can be very demanding, especially at the doctoral level, where few programs accept part-time students. For a PhD program, it might make better sense to borrow money for living expenses and pay it back later from your increased earnings. Seek guidance from your faculty adviser or another knowledgeable person about how much debt it is reasonable to assume.

Remember that the *apparent* costs of graduate education are usually larger than you have to pay. Few doctoral students have to pay tuition. Instead, programs offer financial assistance in the form of tuition scholarships and stipends in return for teaching assistance or research assistance.

How does a MOLECULAR BIOLOGIST . . .

Get to be a SCIENCE POLICY ADVISER?

Early in her career, Patricia Hoben had no doubt that she wanted to be a scientist, but she also wanted to make her work broadly useful. Except for brief stints teaching in a college and a high school, her early trajectory pointed toward a traditional (and distinguished) academic position: a BA in molecular, cellular, and developmental biology at the University of Colorado followed by a PhD in molecular biophysics and biochemistry at Yale and postdoctoral training at the University of California, San Francisco.

"In the early and middle 70s," says Dr. Hoben, "academe was the only respectable track for a PhD biologist. But when I was at San Francisco, one of my friends heard that scientists could get fellowships to do some exciting work in Washington. This was brand new to me; no one at the institution mentioned any opportunities outside the laboratory."

She not only went to Washington; she flourished there. Delighted to find that her analytic skills and scientific knowledge were valued in the public-policy arena, she worked at the US Congress's Office of Technology Assessment and for the assistant secretary of health, providing scientific advice that helped decision-makers to draft regulations, write legis-

continued

lation, and make other decisions about biotechnology and health issues.

"In both these positions I needed the analytical skills I learned from my PhD work, but I also needed a variety of people skills I didn't learn in school. In policy work, I bring in experts who know all the details, but often they don't know how to present themselves to the nontechnical people who will make the political decisions. There's just a tremendous need for people who can bridge these two cultures.

"My PhD was absolutely necessary to my career. There's no other way to get that intensity of training, and no one would take me seriously if I didn't have one. But I equally needed the people skills and patience. In the 'real' world, outside academe, you may be working with people who don't know as much as you do, but they have something to contribute that is needed by the project, and you have to value them for their contribution. You can't be arrogant and expect to bring about change."

The hectic pace of work ("seven days and seven nights a week") and the arrival of children eventually led to a change. After several years of pursuing a long-held interest in public science education as a grant-program director at the Howard Hughes Medical Institute, Dr. Hoben and her family moved to Minneapolis, where she now holds two half-time positions. In one, funded partly by Hughes, she is working with the National Research Council's RISE (Regional Initiatives in Science Education) project to stimulate reform in science education. In the other, she directs a research program for the Minnesota Public Utilities Commission to investigate claims by farmers that electromagnetic radiation affects the milk production and health of dairy cows.

"Public-policy work isn't for everyone, and it isn't easy to find. A more important question for students is, 'Are you preparing to make yourself useful?' For example, on the dairy-cow project, I have a physicist, an electrical engineer, an epidemiologist, an animal physiologist, and a veterinarian all looking at the possibility that electricity affects dairy cows. This is the kind of thing students could be doing to explore career options *and* serve their community—find an interesting problem, team up with students from other disciplines that bear on the problem, and go out and solve it. We're moving into a time when scientists need to be more collaborative and responsive to public interests. I can tell you that the people on this dairy team have never had more fun in their lives than working together and studying this problem."

Deciding Where to Attend Graduate School

Once you feel strongly that a career in science or engineering is for you, it is time to start thinking about where to apply for graduate school. You commonly apply to a specific department or program rather than to the institution as a whole, so you need to pay more attention to the strength of individual departments than to the overall strength of the university.

If you think you want a PhD, the department where you get your degree makes a great deal of difference to your career opportunities. Recent PhDs often receive jobs largely on the basis of where and under whom they earned their degrees. The source of a master's degree can also be important, especially in opening career opportunities. Master's programs with strong thesis or internship possibilities can sometimes lead directly to employers or careers. And just as an alumni network can be an important source of career and job-hunting advice, so can the reputation of the school that those alumni represent influence their ability to find you a job. Through a disciplinary society, library, or guidance office, you can find sources that describe the programs of various universities, such as the American Chemical Society's Directory of Graduate Research (ACS 1994).

The prominence of a department depends largely on the quality of its faculty. Find out as much as you can about specific faculty members; arrange a personal meeting if possible. Do any faculty work on problems that interest or excite you? Do you feel comfortable with those faculty members? If you do not want to work with the faculty in your primary field of interest, you should probably avoid that school. A good source of information is the National Research Council report *Research-Doctorate Programs in the United States: Continuity and Change* (OSEP 1995), which provides national ratings of the quality of program faculty and other information about the characteristics of research-doctorate programs.

Every graduate program has a different educational focus; try to find the one that matches your interests. If you are planning a PhD, select an environment where you think you will be happy for 5 years or even longer. If you are interested in a career outside academe, you might want to go to a graduate school that is ranked lower in research but has internship opportunities and a high rate of success in placing its graduates in industry. Another option is to work for a complementary degree in education, law, or business after your science or engineering degree. Because science is becoming more and more interdisciplinary, programs known for their educational breadth might provide excellent preparation, especially if your goals are unclear. When you join a broad-based program, such as environmental engineering, you might have more potential advisers from whom to choose. Note that some degrees, such as a business master's, can be obtained via distance learning or through "executive degrees" that are offered on weekends. Therefore, the location of a desirable university might not be as important as it was in the past.

You can learn more about a department from a personal visit than from reading or second-hand inquiry. You will probably have to limit visits to your top choices or even wait until you are admitted. But weigh the trouble involved against the magnitude of the investment in time and money that you are about to make. Find out as much as you can before you go, especially about faculty who might be potential advisers. Clarify the requirements for a degree, which vary among schools. When you are there, talk to as many students and professors as possible, in both formal and informal settings. Some universities will help to finance such a visit.

Start investigating potential schools at least a year before you plan to start graduate school. That is when a good relationship with undergraduate advisers can pay off. They can help you to decide on desirable departments and to craft application letters and essays. Ideally, your adviser will know the reputations of faculty at several departments and can make phone calls or other contacts on your behalf. If your adviser does not help, work with your college counselors, seek out graduates and current students of the program, and try to make a personal visit yourself.

Here are some questions that you might want to consider:

➤ What are your career goals, and what school fits them best?

➤ Does that school offer an opportunity to obtain a broad education, including the acquisition of career skills outside your primary field (e.g., a mathematics major might want to take some engineering or physics classes).

➤ Are you comfortable with the size of the program?

➤ Is the department oriented to the needs of its graduate students?

➤ Are you likely to be accepted?

➤ What types of financial support are available?

➤ If you intend a master's degree, is the program endorsed by likely employers?

➤ Does the program have internships or other options

to introduce you to a range of job possibilities?

➤ Are all students required to be teaching assistants? If so, for how long?

➤ What proportion of students who begin the program complete it?

➤ How long does it take most students to obtain a degree?

➤ Are there openings in research groups you would like to join? (These might be competitive in prestigious institutions; an external fellowship provides you with an advantage in entering in such a group: your research is already funded.)

➤ How many women or minority-group students are in the program? What percentage graduate? Where do they go? It helps, especially if you are a woman or minority-group student, to consult the appropriate grapevine for up-to-date advice from peers.

You should also find out what you can about how well a department advises students about their careers. Does it track the careers of former students and make the information available? Does it help their graduates to find positions? Be aware that some graduate programs prepare their students only for academic careers, some direct their students primarily toward industry, and others value academe and industry equally. And some institutions provide good career services, whereas others expect candidates to search out opportunities on their own. Even if you will not be in the job market for several years, you need to investigate such questions before selecting your graduate school.

Applying to graduate school is much more interactive than applying to an undergraduate program. The number of applicants will be much lower, and you will have more opportunities to meet with potential faculty and otherwise influence the application process.

Incorporate samples of your work into your application, including examples of research experience. Evidence of independent study shows the kind of initiative valued by graduate faculty. Solicit as many letters of recommendation as you can (three or four is usually the minimum), and educate the letter-writers about your character and motivation. If possible, visit the program; this allows you to see its facilities and sample the community of people with whom you will be spending the next few years of your life.

Graduate School

Many scientists and engineers say that their time in graduate school was the best experience of their life; others say that it was the worst. The difference often has to do with how much and how early they learned to gain control over their progress. Can you see where you are headed? Can you visualize (and describe) how your research topic or goal fits within the broader themes of your field and society as a whole? Will it lead to further work of importance? Planning, sound guidance, and a focus on setting and achieving goals can make your work meaningful and your life easier.

This section offers advice on survival skills and on ways to enjoy graduate school. If you are struggling, remember that you do not have to struggle alone. Make contacts everywhere. Join and be active in professional associations. Ask for and listen to advice. You will find that many others have also struggled and are pleased to share the lessons they have learned. Look at other people's work, and invite them to

How does a HIGH SCHOOL CHEMISTRY TEACHER . . .

Get to be a RESEARCH CHEMIST and then

an EDUCATIONAL CONSULTANT?

The path of Carol Balfe's career illustrates that it is sometimes not very useful to stick to a blueprint. After a series of very substantial—and unplanned—changes, her present occupation makes use of virtually all her experiences and allows her to do work that she values highly: trying to reform science education on a national scale.

As a young woman, Dr. Balfe joined a Catholic order and began teaching high school chemistry. After a year, she was sent to get a PhD at the University of Wisconsin; instead, she decided to leave the order to return to teaching.

"I taught for 12 years altogether," she says, "in a Catholic school, a suburban school in Illinois, an inner-city school in Vallejo, California, and a school for dropouts. I recognized that teachers didn't know very well how to motivate students because they spent most of their lives either going to school or teaching school. I decided to put my money where my mouth was and get some real-world experience."

She began with a master's degree in chemistry and biochemistry, and then at the age of 36 entered the PhD program in inorganic chemistry at the University of California,

continued

Berkeley. "By then I had a little more 'street smarts' and world wisdom. My future husband worked for the Department of Employment, so I was very aware of labor market issues. I got fired up to do the research I hadn't finished at Wisconsin, but I was keeping the education issues in the back of my mind."

After earning her PhD, she spent two years at Sandia National Laboratories, where she was one of only two chemists on a team of materials scientists. "This was an opportunity for cross-disciplinary learning you seldom find in academe." Then she returned to the Bay Area, where she was offered a job by Raychem, a materials-science company. "I had wanted to work in industry to learn as much as I could. In graduate school I was told that industry is where the second-rate people go, but that's not true. You can go as deeply as you want in research. But beyond that, industry has different intellectual challenges, personal challenges, the opportunity to exploit a wider variety of your talents."

She continued her interest in education by doing volunteer work. Raychem was helping the schools of East Palo Alto by donating computers, but the equipment was unfamiliar to the teachers. "This was too early in computers. Instead of trying to teach the classes ourselves, we should have been listening to the teachers, finding out what they needed so that we could be a resource for them."

In 1993, her husband died; after a leave from Raychem, her mentor there suggested that it was time for her to tackle the educational mission that she had been contemplating for so long.

"He just stopped me in my tracks; he saw it more clearly than I did. He offered me 3 months' company time to figure it out. I talked and listened and networked with people everywhere. Now I'm out on my own. What I want to do is to leverage my talent and background to make a significant difference in precollege education, especially for children of color and girls. In particular, I want to help industries and professional societies have more effective and strategic roles in public science education.

"This may sound like a 'grand plan,' that I knew all along how I'd bring all my careers together. But the truth is that I have always taken one little step at a time, according to what felt right.

"The most important message I have for graduate students is that you don't have to make all your career decisions now. First, get a solid background and learn to pay attention to what feels right. When you are ready, doors will open. The world needs people who can translate from one highly specialized world to another. Careers that combine interests and expertise are the careers of the 21st century."

look at yours. The more you interact with others, the more you will learn.

Choosing a Degree

How does a master's degree differ from a PhD? Jules LaPidus, president of the Council of Graduate Schools, offers a comparison: "A student must be able to understand and use knowledge at the master's level and make significant contributions to it at the doctoral level" (Peters 1992).

At the master's level, you will gain knowledge on subjects not usually covered in undergraduate programs. Students are generally required to take courses for 1 or 2 years and sometimes required to write a thesis and take departmental examinations. After successfully completing the examinations, you can take a master's degree and enter the workplace or proceed into a PhD program.

Knowledge at the master's level is intended to prepare you to practice a profession (such as engineering, environmental studies, business, information science, or biotechnology) or to continue on to more advanced study. A PhD program might be necessary if you want to do research and teach at the university level (CGS 1989).

In many disciplines, especially in the physical sciences, master's degrees are earned on the way to the PhD. Some students who do not complete the PhD settle for a master's, (Peters 1992; Tobias et al. 1995). But most master's degrees are considered professional degrees—sometimes called the professional master's—and are highly valued in traditional fields, such as engineering and nursing, as well as in newer fields, such as microbiology, bioengineering, computer science, and environmental studies (Tobias et al. 1995). A professional master's might teach such specific skills as instru-

Choosing a Degree

Wesley has just passed his departmental examinations in chemistry. He enjoys classwork and laboratory work equally. His grades are average, but he has excellent "people skills," which make him a popular student teacher and mentor of local high-school science students.

He has difficulty in envisioning a career beyond graduate school, and he prefers not to spend all his time in the laboratory. A friend suggests that he might want to reconsider his goal of a PhD in favor of a master's. His faculty adviser shows no enthusiasm for any option but the PhD.

➤ What options does he have if he stops at a master's degree?

➤ How important is it that his adviser will not discuss alternatives?

See Appendix A for a discussion of this scenario.

mentation design, project management, systems integration, counseling, solving of complex problems, and risk analysis. Those skills are often enhanced by internships or field work. The MS degree involves less commitment and time than a PhD, but it can lead to careers with greater responsibility and higher pay than a BS alone (CGS 1989). It is also useful for those who want to teach in high schools and community colleges. The granting of master's degrees in many fields of science and engineering is increasing rapidly (although entry-level MS programs might not be available in many sciences) (Bloom 1995).

Beyond the master's level, the most-common professional science-oriented degree is the MD (CGS 1989). Students might decide to enter medicine from the bachelor's level or after a master's in a related field, such as bioengineering or nursing. Other professional degrees that might be relevant to science are the doctor of law (JD), doctor of public health (DPH), doctor of education (EdD), and doctor of library science (DLS) (Peters 1992). A popular hybrid degree is the MD/PhD, which takes about 3 more years than an MD and provides training in research not offered in most MD programs.

In science and engineering, however, a research PhD is the norm at the doctoral level. A doctoral program is usually an apprenticeship consisting of lecture or laboratory courses, seminars, examinations, discussions, independent study, research, and teaching. After passing departmental examinations, the student enters candidacy under the supervision of a faculty adviser and a dissertation committee. Candidacy is a period for performing original research, writing a dissertation describing that research, and orally defending the dissertation before the faculty committee. Candidacy normally lasts 2-4 years; this period has increased in recent decades (Peters 1992). The traditional goal of a PhD scientist or engineer is research or teaching at a university, industrial laboratory, or government agency, although it is common to progress to other positions and even careers.

The PhD might not be the end of your study. In some fields, most academic jobs (even in 4-year institutions) now require a year or more of postdoctoral experience (see later section on "Postdoctoral Study").

To help you to think through degree options, gather written descriptions of various programs and, when possible, talk with students, faculty, and graduates of the ones that appeal to you. Sometimes, there are excellent opportunities abroad, especially postdoctoral appointments. In addition, distance learning programs—in which courses are taken via satellite, videotape, television, or computer—are increasingly popular and provide an additional option. Because fields differ so widely, there is no substitute for firsthand information from people in your own discipline.

Choosing an Adviser

Finding a faculty adviser (or major professor) is often the most important step in your graduate career. There is no substitute for guidance from someone who has already survived what you are attempting and who can offer wise perspective on how best to match your talents with an appropriate career. What kind of adviser should you look for? The ideal person can not only guide your career, support your research, and help to find you a job, but can also serve as a close and caring mentor—a "research uncle," as one author puts it. Obviously, this is a rare combination, but one worth searching for. Discovering such a person while you are still an undergraduate might be reason enough to select the university where he or she works.

If you arrive at graduate school without having chosen an adviser, which is commonly the case, start looking right away. Look up publications of faculty in your department; talk with support staff and professors. If possible, track down past and present students who have worked with a particular adviser. Some programs have laboratory rotation courses that will allow you to work part-time and try out several different professors.

Do you need a prominent scientist as an adviser? Prestige is important, because you will want expert guidance on your research and help in finding a job when you are finished. But you need a person who is available, who values interacting with you and other students, and who is willing to teach necessary survival skills.

Ask about the laboratory group that your potential adviser has assembled. Has the adviser secured adequate funding for the group? Does the group have off-campus, collaborative interactions with other academic or industrial groups? Look for postdoctoral researchers and advanced graduate students in the group who can help you when the adviser is busy. See whether nearby laboratory groups share research seminars with yours and will extend the breadth of your experience.

When you choose an adviser, discuss important issues early. Be frank about your plans, your strengths, and your weak points. Where do you need help? What abilities can you offer? What commitments will be expected of you? If you will work as part of a research team, how will your role be defined and how will you gain credit for your own contribution to the team's work? Will your advisor support a nonresearch or nonacademic career choice? Raise such questions before they grow into problems.

It is very important to remember that the education of a graduate student is the responsibility of an entire department, not just of a single adviser. Take the initiative early to form a thesis committee. Discuss your project and your status with committee members and other faculty as you go along. Consider asking two people to be your advisers, perhaps as co-chairs of your dissertation committee: one might have a high level of expertise, and the other might have more time to meet with you. This is particularly important if your topic is interdisciplinary. Every professional contact that you

How does a NUCLEAR ENGINEER . . .

Get to be a THERAPEUTIC RADIATION PHYSICIST?

In 1976, Bill Edge had earned an MS in nuclear engineering at the Georgia Institute of Technology and was working on his doctorate when a friend called to offer him a position at a hospital. A hospital?

"I'd done some work at Oak Ridge in health physics," says Mr. Edge, "which is really a safety area—making sure people aren't exposed to radioactivity. But most health physics jobs were in nuclear reactors, and after Three Mile Island they just weren't being built any more. And I wanted to do something more interesting and more useful. So I moved over to the medical area. I have a good bit of clinical contact with patients, so I know I am doing something useful, and the work gets more interesting all the time."

For the last 13 years, he has been director of the radiation-physics department at Northeast Georgia Medical Center in Gainesville. His work includes planning computerized radiation treatments, making physics measurements on equipment used to treat patients, and serving as a liaison between physicians, dosimetrists, and therapists. As radiation safety officer, he also ensures the safety of the treatment machines and generates tables to be used in treatment calculations. Now he is preparing to accept a three-dimen-

continued

sional planning system that uses data from computed tomography to plan patient treatments with 3-D graphics presentation of patient anatomy and treatment beams.

Mr. Edge is technically a therapeutic radiation physicist, which represents a combination of radiation physics and medical therapy. This is distinct from a radiation therapist, who administers treatment to patients, and a radiation oncologist, who is an MD who has overall responsibility for patients' treatment. He does not feel that a PhD is necessary for his work; instead, the essential degree is a master's in physics, ideally accompanied by one of the programs accredited by the American Association of Physicists in Medicine (AAPM). These programs, most of them offered at large teaching hospitals, combine classroom and clinical work.

"You can get into this field the way I did: Work under someone who is already certified as a therapeutic radiation physicist and gain your experience on the job. But one way or another you need the right medical background. And that's where the AAPM programs are just right."

"I have also found that certification is an asset in this field. After working for 3 years, a medical physicist is eligible to stand for boards in his area, such as therapy physics, diagnostic physics, or nuclear medicine physics. I am presently board certified by the American Board of Radiology (ABR), the American Board of Medical Physics (ABMP), and the American Board of Science in Nuclear Medicine (ABSNM). Most of the job listings today are requesting board certification, and some fields, such as mammography, are requiring certification in order to do equipment calibrations."

make strengthens your standing and raises your chances of building a rewarding career.

The Adviser–Student Relationship

In many fields of science and engineering, especially in a PhD program, you might be invited to work as a research assistant in your adviser's research program. An aspect of this research might become your own research topic. Usually such an arrangement benefits both parties: you, as a "scholar's apprentice," gain original research experience, and the professor gains much-needed assistance.

If you are invited to work on such a program, find out as much as you can about it in advance. Try to get a feel for whether you will be encouraged to educate yourself broadly enough. Many students focus their energies so narrowly on a specific aspect of research that they neglect to understand the context of their work or to develop the skills that make an interdisciplinary career possible.

Make a special effort to understand how your adviser will award credit for the work you do. For example, will your name be listed first on any publications resulting from your own work? That is especially important on a joint project, where your own contributions might be hard to distinguish from those of others. You do not want to end up without a portfolio that you can use to start a new career or laboratory of your own. Review another document from COSEPUP (*On Being a Scientist: Responsible Conduct in Research*) that provides guidance on research ethics (COSEPUP 1995). Read this booklet over before you begin research activities; encourage a panel discussion on the topic via one of the mechanisms discussed here.

What kind of relationship will you have with your ad-

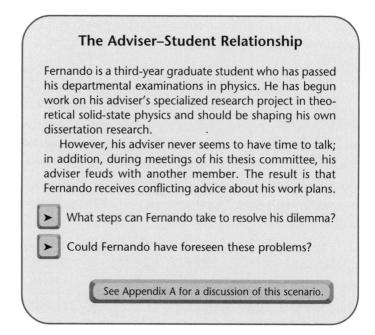

The Adviser–Student Relationship

Fernando is a third-year graduate student who has passed his departmental examinations in physics. He has begun work on his adviser's specialized research project in theoretical solid-state physics and should be shaping his own dissertation research.

However, his adviser never seems to have time to talk; in addition, during meetings of his thesis committee, his adviser feuds with another member. The result is that Fernando receives conflicting advice about his work plans.

➤ What steps can Fernando take to resolve his dilemma?

➤ Could Fernando have foreseen these problems?

See Appendix A for a discussion of this scenario.

viser: teacher–student? employer–employee? Will you be colleagues or adversaries—in school and beyond? It is primarily a professional relationship, but it is also a personal one. It will succeed only if both sides are willing to work at it. It is most likely to succeed if your major professor is someone whose standards and goals appeal to you and who has a special interest in you as a person. The best outcome is that your adviser turns out to be a true mentor—a wise and trusted counselor.

There is often an implicit contract between adviser and student: the adviser devotes time, guidance, and personal energy in the expectation that the student-apprentice will some day do research that will make the mentor proud. Does your adviser have this expectation? Do you? Can the two of you discuss other career possibilities as well?

What can you do if the relationship with your adviser is a poor one? If the two of you cannot work it out, you should try to find another professor who is qualified and willing to take you on. In general, it is best to make a change as soon as you see that the situation is unworkable. Will changing advisers slow your progress? Will you have to alter the direction of your research? Only if it is late in your student career should you endure a difficult situation rather than try for a better one. The head of the graduate program or the department chair might be able to help you to decide what to do and who might help you.

You might decide to seek several advisers to broaden the range of counsel available to you. That is particularly important for women and minority-group students, who might wish to have a woman or member of their minority group as a mentor.

Choosing a Research Topic

Along with choosing an adviser, the most important decision you will make in graduate school is choosing a research topic. You will likely spend a number of years, and possibly the rest of your career, working in the general field that you select now.

You might be tempted to tackle something ambitious that will win a big prize. Resist that temptation. This is the beginning of your career. The point of graduate school is to learn to do research. Be aware that your original topic, especially in the life sciences, might not work out. A good thesis adviser will have backup plans in case your original project fails to yield results.

Your topic should be original, and it should advance what is known about your field. But it should be something

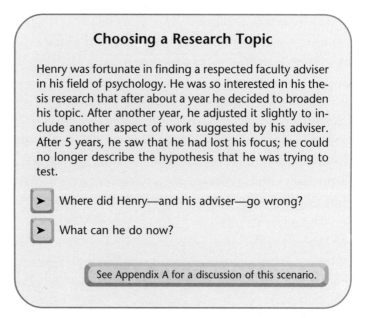

Choosing a Research Topic

Henry was fortunate in finding a respected faculty adviser in his field of psychology. He was so interested in his thesis research that after about a year he decided to broaden his topic. After another year, he adjusted it slightly to include another aspect of work suggested by his adviser. After 5 years, he saw that he had lost his focus; he could no longer describe the hypothesis that he was trying to test.

➤ Where did Henry—and his adviser—go wrong?

➤ What can he do now?

See Appendix A for a discussion of this scenario.

that you and your adviser believe you can complete and write up in about 2 years, for an MS, or 3 years, for a PhD. When you enter the next stage of your career, you can advance to another aspect of the topic if it still interests you.

When thinking about your topic, imagine how to describe it with the perspective required of a dissertation. Think of a title, a summary, the kinds of conclusions that you might reach. A dissertation should not only describe your work, but also explain its relevance to previous research and its importance in extending the general understanding of the topic.

Ask yourself the toughest questions you can think of: Will this research get your career off to a strong start? Is the subject vitally interesting to you? Is this field becoming more active? Will you have financial support, whether from a professor's research grant or from some other source? Will you learn important methods that you will be able to apply to other problems of interest? Can you complete your work in a reasonable amount of time?

Those are indeed tough questions, and it is unrealistic to expect a yes on all of them. The point is to gain a realistic picture of your research environment. Remember also that your overall field of research is more important than the specific subfield that you might explore in school. The techniques and principles learned in graduate school will serve you well even as you move to new subfields or specialties.

Think of your work also as a contribution to the community. Will your work stimulate that of your colleagues? How can you apply their results to your own? Can you imagine how to collaborate with them on a larger project? Your research topic should make sense in the context of a journey that you will undertake in the company of others.

Achieving Breadth

Your main focus in graduate school is to learn the fundamentals of your discipline, but you also want to broaden your competence and acquire other career skills that can enhance your value to employers. Breadth can be described under two categories—academic and career.

For academic breadth, both master's-degree and doctoral-degree recipients should have some familiarity with one or more subfields. For example, a chemist might benefit from courses in biology or computer science or from an internship with industry. Such breadth might allow you to see your own work in a fuller context and understand interdisciplinary questions.

We have discussed how easy it is to overspecialize in pursuing a research topic. An overnarrow "field of view" might slow your recognition of emerging fields of research, limit your later research contributions, or restrict your career options. A strong argument can be made for taking nonscience courses that enhance your competences, such as courses in business or management. That is most easily done in your undergraduate years, but even if done in graduate school the extra effort will pay off later in qualifying you to manage or lead. For example, it might be important to achieve a thorough grounding in statistics and experimental design, especially if you contemplate a career in industry, where controlled experiments are often not possible and experiments are very expensive because they are commonly done on production-scale equipment.

You can achieve breadth through dual degrees or "strong" minors. For example, you might obtain a degree in mechanical engineering at the bachelor's level but decide to focus on aerospace engineering at the master's level. Employers often support such study financially because it brings them needed expertise; with such support, you might be able to study part-time, in the evening, or by distance learning.

Some engineering students pursue a degree in another field in combination with the master's in engineering. A master's in management of technology, taught by engineering schools, can be valuable for those who aspire to management positions in a technical company. A master's in business administration (MBA) teaches the basics of management, finance, human resources, and accounting—valuable skills that can help you to advance both inside and outside your company.

Career breadth is attained through such activities as internships and on-campus research centers that work in col-

How does a NURSE . . .

Get to be a RESEARCH MANAGER?

As a young single mother of two, Diana Garcia-Prichard worked as a nurse to support her family. But she signed up for chemistry courses at California State University at Hayward, and she felt her life shift. "Physical science was perfectly suited to my thought processes," she says. "It was the first time in my life that I found something I really wanted to do."

She completed her BS *cum laude*, entered graduate school at the University of Rochester, and in 4.5 years had a master's and a PhD in chemical physics. She was hired as a research scientist by Eastman Kodak Company, where she is a senior research scientist who also supervises technology-development projects.

"In grad school I knew I wanted to do research, and I thought I would become a professor and help my community back home in California. But my adviser told me it was too difficult for women to get grants or academic jobs. I didn't have the experience to know there were grants for minorities, and my adviser didn't know it. Fortunately I've had a wonderful research experience here. And Kodak, being a big company, has been able to support some of my other goals."

continued

Dr. Garcia-Prichard has worked hard to reform science policy and education, serving on the Clinton-Gore transition team, the National Science Foundation Education and Human Resources Directorate, an American Chemical Society editorial board, and the board of a local community college.

"I want students today to be better informed than I was about careers. For example, they need to know what kinds of grants there are, and who can get them. Also, there's a huge gap between what students learn in universities and what's needed in an industry workplace. Here I work in physical chemistry, but I also have to be able to collaborate with materials scientists, engineers, and chemists.

"And they should know that the corporate environment is changing today. Shareholders are forcing corporations to downsize staff, but the work still has to get done.

"Choosing the right adviser can help—someone who not only is a good scientist, but is savvy about careers and understands what you need. If you pick a famous scientist who is not a good caregiver, you end up staying in school too long and doing a lot of their work. I was done in 4.5 years, and part of the reason was that I stood up to my adviser. I told him, if you want someone to do your lab work, you'll have to find someone else. I'm here for a chemistry degree, not a degree in plumbing."

That bold approach will not always be successful. The best advice in dealing with an adviser is to be honest, persistent, and communicative. Because your goals and those of your faculty adviser are not usually the same, a good relationship requires continued effort, good judgment, and good will—on both sides.

laboration with industry. Internships with industry or government laboratories take time away from campus-based research or classes. But they can lead to broader perspectives, new contacts, and better jobs. They can also help you to mature and develop confidence in your ability to succeed in the nonacademic world. Taken together, these effects might paradoxically *shorten* the total time spent in school.

You can also benefit from extending your breadth of career skills, such as those discussed in Chapter 3. For example, students with good communication ability—who can describe their work to nonspecialists—might prove adept at working in teams of people from industry or other disciplines.

Ensuring Steady Progress

How long does it take to finish graduate school? A nonthesis master's degree usually requires 1-2 years, a thesis master's 2-3 years (it is common to take extra time if you also hold a job). The time between receipt of the bachelors' degree and receipt of the PhD varies widely according to field. Check the latest date at the NRC's *Career Planning Center For Beginning Scientists and Engineers* and ask recent graduates at your institution how long it has taken them.

For a PhD candidate, working expeditiously is important. Increases in degree times are generally undesirable and often imply that students are not making the best use of their time. Slow progress might mean that someone has become too comfortable in the educational environment, isn't properly motivated to find answers, or has bogged down in techniques. Some corporations, postdoctoral-fellowship boards, and university faculty-search committees use time to degree as an indicator of a student's initiative and drive, and it influences their decision about whether to invite a student for interviews.

Check the average time to degree at the program you are considering. Try to choose an adviser with a reputation for moving students along. Set a schedule to meet regularly with your adviser and dissertation committee. Even if your finish date is hard for you to predict, keep your committee up to date and solicit its advice.

If your thesis work does not involve you with others, join or form a dissertation support group. Giving talks and exchanging critiques with trusted peers—say, once a week or once a month—can help to keep you moving, extend your contacts, and moderate the intensity of solitary scholarship. Reach out to other students, postdoctoral researchers, and faculty. The presence and empathy of others can make your graduate years both more gratifying and more productive.

Also, do not forget that most universities have counseling centers that can offer a sympathetic ear. They can work with you and perhaps your adviser to develop a less-stressful environment for you.

Postdoctoral Study

In some fields, such as biology and chemistry, postdoctoral appointments are virtually required for an academic career. In other fields, such as engineering, they are uncommon. Postdoctoral appointments are short-term appointments (usually 1 or more years) with universities, research institutions, government, or industry in which you have the opportunity to gain in-depth research skills. They are more commonly used to prepare for a career in academe than for a career in industry, although the latter is becoming more common. When you take a postdoctoral appointment in a field different from that of your dissertation, it can provide increased breadth and improve employment prospects.

Many postdoctoral openings are advertised in the scientific journals, but many are not. As soon as you know that you want to try for one, put out feelers among your contacts and alert your faculty allies that you need help in finding the right position. Remember that although many positions are in academe, you can also find them in national laboratories, in industry, in research laboratories, in the federal government, and elsewhere.

For example, a government agency might have a major postdoctoral-fellowship program that can constitute a good mechanism for you to move from a general background in chemistry to one in environmental chemistry. If you are interested in nonacademic employment, such a position can broaden your possibilities and ease your transition into a nonacademic culture. There are also nonresearch postdoctoral positions, offered primarily by disciplinary societies, in which you can gain experience in public policy and other fields.

When academic jobs are scarce, students might find themselves taking successive postdoctoral positions—as many as three or four—while they wait for a permanent position. The danger of extending postdoctoral study is that you might become stuck in a series of temporary appointments. Getting yet another postdoctoral appointment at an institution does not mean that that institution will offer you a job. It might be better to accept a job with less prestige than you had hoped for so that your "real" career can begin. If there is no job offer, you might be able to use—or decide to add—new skills to find a position in a related field.

Before accepting a postdoctoral appointment, ask your contacts how effective the supervisors at the postdoctoral site are in developing the skills and promoting the careers of its scientists. Ask former postdoctoral researchers of that site what ideas they were allowed to take with them to use in starting their own independent research projects.

For postdoctoral fellows, career guidance is a pressing issue. Too often they exist in a state of "peerlessness," sometimes not even knowing whether there are other postdoctoral appointees in their program. When possible, seek out and interact with other postdoctoral appointees and establish a committee of several faculty members or other established scientists who are willing to play a role in your training.

The issue of guidance becomes critical when the time comes to search for a permanent position. Many postdoctoral researchers describe a dismaying inability to locate job openings and connect with potential employers. Because so many jobs at the postdoctoral level are arranged by word of mouth, the network of contacts that you have built through your school years becomes more important than ever.

If you are fortunate enough to have to choose between a postdoctoral appointment and a job, ask yourself several questions. Will the appointment allow you to complete important research that you probably would not have time to do on the job? Can you take the postdoctoral appointment before moving to the job, or is the job likely to disappear before you finish it? Learn as much as you can about your prospects of securing other available positions in light of anticipated market conditions.

Some Tips for Foreign Students

If you are coming to a graduate school in the United States from another country, careful planning can help you to avoid some common frustrations.

For example, living expenses are almost always higher than you expect. No matter how your fellowship is described, expect it not to cover all your expenses.

Understand the conditions of your visa. Whether or not you decide to stay in the United States after your studies, find out how long you would be allowed to stay for practical training. If you are here for a PhD, you might want to complete the master's, take a year off for practical training in industry, and then return to complete the PhD.

Find out beforehand how much credit you will receive for courses already taken. Misunderstandings are common, so get agreements in writing. For example, will the master's degree from your home-country university be recognized, or will you have to do it over? Each university has its own standards.

Select your research topic, and especially your adviser, with care. This is the person who will have the biggest direct influence on your life as a graduate student. Check out the reputation of potential advisers with fellow students. If you need special coursework or assistance in adjusting to a different culture, does the adviser seem ready to help?

Network early and continually. It is easy to become isolated in a single department, especially if you are a foreign student with perhaps limited communication skills. Make an effort to integrate with American students. Whether or not you decide to stay in the United States after your studies, participate in professional organizations and make connections that will be beneficial to you here or at home. Join other university or community activities, such as foreign-student associations.

Be aware that your choice of courses is probably greater than you think. It is easy to become buried in your specialty and lose out on a wide selection of topics—such as management, law, business, and music—that might help you to understand the context of your work or simply enrich you as a person.

Learn to use the library and other research aids as early as possible. You can work much more efficiently when you know where and how to get quickly to sources of good information.

After School, What Next?

Don't wait until the last minute to start making final decisions about your future. These might include choosing a postdoctoral position, seeking yet more education, or looking for employment in either academic or nonacademic sectors. A good rule of thumb is to start thinking and searching in earnest about a year before your likely graduation date.

A good deal of time might have passed since you began graduate school. Think again about some of the items discussed in Chapter 2. You are more mature now, and you certainly know a great deal more about what it would be like to be a professor. Look honestly at the employment market for different fields, using information provided by the NRC in its Internet *Career Planning Center For Beginning Scientists and Engineers*, your disciplinary society, and government agencies, such as the National Science Foundation and the National Institutes of Health. Reflect on what you want in your work life *and* your personal life. Will you need additional education (such as an MBA, MD, or JD) to be successful in a given occupation? Are you willing to spend still more time in school? Are you willing to take a low-paying postdoctoral position if that is the norm for your field? Talk to other recent graduates and postdoctoral appointees to learn about their experience in the job market. Do not hesitate to let *everyone* know that you are looking for work. Fruitful connections are often made where least expected.

Action Points

 As an undergraduate, work with your faculty adviser to plan a well-rounded education. Talk with faculty and students in potential graduate and professional programs.

 Discuss potential programs with students and faculty and via Internet bulletin boards.

 At both the undergraduate and graduate levels, take courses outside your major and primary field that you think will be useful in your career.

 Develop a network of contacts, both inside and outside your discipline and both on and off campus, to help you to understand the full range of opportunities available to you.

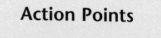 Seek advice from people outside your field as well as inside it.

When evaluating a possible dissertation topic, think of a title, summary, and possible conclusions.

 Look for classes and internships that will increase your breadth and experience.

 When evaluating possible faculty advisers, look for a person who not only is professionally competent, but also cares about the quality of your educational experience.

 To gain perspective on your work, look at other people's projects and invite them to look at yours.

 Plan ways to complete your degree expeditiously.

 At your university or via the Internet, join or form an interdisciplinary dissertation support group or a journal club (in which students and faculty meet to discuss the latest journal articles).

HOW DO YOU GET THE JOB THAT IS RIGHT FOR YOU?

Finding a job takes work; finding the job that you *want* takes hard work. Many recent science and engineering graduates are lucky enough to move into desirable employment immediately. But it's common to spend months or even more than a year in the job search.

Finding a Job

When looking for a position, do not simply rely on the want ads in the scientific journals—although this is definitely the place to begin. Think more broadly. Meetings and conferences are a good way to explore your discipline and to meet numerous people in your field and talk to them about employment— either for a postdoctoral position or a longer-term, "real" job. You might also have the opportunity to demonstrate your research and communication skills (an excellent way is to present a poster or paper) and even to interview for positions.

Be prepared for intense competition for the most-desir-

Finding a Job

Carol has earned a PhD in biology and completed 2 years of postdoctoral work in molecular genetics. She has heard that academic positions are hard to find, so before her postdoc concludes, she applies to several biotechnology firms doing work in her field. She is surprised to be turned down by all of them; several suggest that she seemed somewhat uncommunicative and unfamiliar with "corporate culture."

➤ What might the firms have found lacking in Carol?

➤ How could she have better approached a career in industry?

See Appendix A for a discussion of this scenario.

able positions at leading universities, firms, and government laboratories. As the academic and research job markets have tightened, employers have learned that they can pick from a larger pool of applicants. Will an institution hire a PhD fresh off the campus when it can hire a PhD with 1-4 years of postdoctoral experience?

However, knowing who you are and knowing what a position requires can be more helpful in finding a position than a long list of credentials. Says Richard Bolles, "the people who get hired are not necessarily those who will do the job best, but those who know the most about how to get hired." Finding a job is a learnable skill (Jensen 1995).

Consider everyone you meet along the way as a potential helper. A network of contacts among students, faculty, and friends is the springboard for your job search. Plug in to the alumni networks of your school, college, and even graduate school. You are more likely to hear helpful news about an opening from someone who knows you and likes you than from someone who only sees your name printed on a piece of paper.

The favorite job-hunting tools in this country—resumes, agencies, and advertisements—are seldom effective by themselves. One study found that among companies that received resumes, one job was offered and accepted for every 1,470 resumes that were received (Jensen 1995). Many of the people hiring for these companies are overwhelmed by mass-produced resumes and computer-generated cover letters, all of which make a strong case for their applicant (Tobias et al. 1995).

The Internet is rapidly becoming more interactive and helpful: you can join a newsgroup, trade advice on bulletin boards and make contacts worldwide. You will find many first-person anecdotes about how the job market works— and does not work—as well as tips, queries, complaints, anecdotes, statistics, and advice about such topics as the job search, getting along with your adviser, and forming dissertation support groups. The National Research Council's online *Career Planning Center For Beginning Scientists and Engineers* centralizes job openings, career information, guidance, and links to other forms and sources of information. It also provides a location for you to post your resume online.

Bolles recommends what he calls the "creative" job search. Start, he says, by figuring out your best skills and favorite subjects. Then learn all you can about any employers that interest you. Finally, use your contacts to seek out people who have the power to hire you and arrange to talk with them. He claims that this technique, if used diligently, is the most successful in finding the right job for you. The next best technique is to apply directly to an employer without doing explicit research on the organization—but you should apply in person. This, however, works says Bolles, "only if pursued faithfully over a number of weeks or months." The third-best method, he says, is simply to ask friends for job leads and follow them up diligently (Peters 1992).

There are other ways to increase your chances of making a good match. Do not wait for employers to come knocking: they probably won't. Do what you can to make personal contacts and locate job openings (Tobias et al. 1995). Show creativity in finding opportunities; this alone might impress potential employers.

Your faculty advisers can be enormously helpful in the job search by opening doors, praising your abilities, and suggesting new approaches. They can also help employers to appreciate the qualities of students and how well they might fit particular positions. Familiarize yourself with employment niches revealed by your advisers' contacts and collaborations.

Attend as many job fairs and conventions as you can. There you will find abundant trade literature and a social environment that makes it easier to meet people in your field. National meetings of science and engineering disciplinary societies are where job-seekers can contact employers who have advertised jobs or postdoctoral positions. Even for meetings, prepare to meet with specific people or organizations.

A good starting point is the advertisements in disciplinary-society magazines or professional or general publications, such as the *Chronicle of Higher Education*, *Technology Review*, or *Science*, and newspapers in major science and engineering employment centers, such as Washington, D.C.,

How does a RESEARCH BIOLOGIST . . .

Get to be a HIGH SCHOOL TEACHER?

"I knew very early I wanted to be a teacher," says Toby M. Horn, PhD. "I just forgot for a while."

While she forgot, she got an AB in chemistry and a PhD in biology and did postdoctoral work at Johns Hopkins and the National Cancer Institute. She loved her research, but she knew that something was missing from her life. During a 6-month sabbatical, she became a potter's apprentice and consulted with friends about career paths. *A Nation at Risk* came out, and she remembered what she had started out to do. She took a job at Thomas Jefferson High School for Science and Technology in Virginia. In the state of Virginia, it is possible to obtain certification based on your professional experience with minimal coursework. She has taught more than 3,000 students in 10 years, exposing every incoming freshman to an innovative curriculum featuring hands-on work with biotechnology laboratory methods (e.g., cells, DNA, and proteins). Now she is working to acquaint more high-school teachers with the world of research.

"High-school teaching is not an alternative to academics," she says, "it is its own path. It's really rewarding if you like kids and if you really love science. It's as creative as research, only different, and the rewards can be tremendous.

continued

I give a lecture called 'You haven't failed if you become a high-school teacher.' But it was a hard decision to leave lab life, especially as a woman, because of the stereotype: 'she can't do science so she will teach.'

"The truth is I can do research, and I love it. If I had to do it over, I would definitely get my PhD again. It was a real empowerment for me. Doing scientific research with a goal of a thesis develops a habit of mind. But I realized I had no interest in the standard university path. As I say, I always knew deep down I'd be a teacher."

New York, Boston, Los Angeles, and the Silicon Valley area. Those advertisements not only show you what is available, but also offer a realistic picture of the qualifications that employers expect. These publications and many others can be found via the Internet (and are directly accessible via the National Research Council's online *Career Planning Center For Beginning Scientists and Engineers*).

Interviewing for a Job

You will be doing interviews during this year; take them seriously. You want to impress the people whom you meet that you are the person for the position. That means giving a presentation that is not only substantive but also *interesting*. You are essentially giving a one-person show to busy and knowledgeable people. You might not be able to surprise them, but demonstrate your own grasp of what you have done and your interest in your field. Do not just recite data; tell a story. Be enthusiastic. Be clear. Be brief. Rehearse beforehand with friends and colleagues and listen to their suggestions. Do not be afraid to describe the context of your research: How does it fit into your field, and into society as a whole? Those in your audience who are experts will enjoy hearing your version, and those who are not will be grateful for the perspective.

Another important feature of an interview is the often-asked question: What are your plans? For nonresearch positions, this is often asked as: Where do you want to be 5 years from now? For research positions, you will be expected to describe your plans for research and the contributions that you plan to make to the field. Regardless of what type of position you are looking for, the key to your search is to make the right match: to find your own niche within an organization.

Give special attention to features that can distinguish you from other applicants. Interview dynamics vary greatly between research and nonresearch positions, but in both cases, be specific: How can you make a contribution to the organization?

For research positions, familiarize yourself beforehand with the research interests of the faculty member or the industrial group that you will meet. They will be interested in your research plans. Rehearse your presentation with mentors, laboratory colleagues, fellow students, and anyone else whose opinion you value, and take the time to polish it at meetings and poster sessions during disciplinary-society meetings. Be responsive; ask pertinent questions; answer questions confidently and difficult questions honestly. Do not be afraid to say, "That's a very good question. The experiment hasn't been done, but thank you for the idea. I'll let you know what happens." Postinterview thanks and followups are critical.

For nonresearch positions, a formal research presentation probably will not be required. Instead, you will probably be invited to an all-day interview in which you will speak with potential supervisors and fellow employees. Those you speak with will be looking for a match between you and the organization: What skills, knowledge, and experience can you contribute that are not already present?

At the same time, remember that this is *your* interview. Ask the people you speak with what their workday is like; try to imagine yourself working there. This is your chance to find out whether the organization and the type of work that they do constitute a good match for you as well.

How you handle an interview tells potential employers not only what you know, but also how well you communicate and present yourself. They are seeing you as a potential employee dealing with the same kinds of stressful situations that you might be expected to handle on the job (Tobias et al. 1995). Use informational interviews to find out about particular universities or industries.

In the case of doctoral or postdoctoral candidates, learn the considerable differences between interviewing for industry and for academe. For a research position, both will scrutinize the depth of your research presentation, your teaching experience and skills, how well you work with others, your research plans, and your list of publications. But an industrial interviewer will pay close attention to how you will fit as a member of a team in the corporate culture. Any employer will want you to explain how valuable you can be as a scientist or engineer in a variety of positions.

Some foreign students seeking employment face the added difficulty of applying and interviewing in a second language. A mastery of the language becomes doubly important when teaching, networking, and communicating your work to nonexperts are components of employment. In most cases, there is no substitute for mastering English to demonstrate your knowledge of your subject.

If you are already in a university that does not offer formal instruction in how to prepare for a job interview, you can take constructive steps on your own. Use the many books available, including those listed in the bibliography in this guide. Prepare a list of questions that your prospective employer might ask you, and then prepare answers and rehearse them aloud. Seek out fellow students who have been through the interviewing process or supportive faculty and ask them to conduct a mock interview with you and give you comments.

Finding a Job Is Hard Work

Prepare for possible disappointment before it comes. Many bright young job-seekers have never failed or been rejected in an academic setting. You might have been a star in high school and college and made it to the graduate school of your choice. But the harsh realities of a job search can deal severe blows to self-esteem (Tobias et al. 1995).

Robert L. Peters, in *Getting What You Came For* (1992), offers a helpful summary of guidelines:

➤ Start thinking as early as you can about where you might work. Once you have your degree, start looking immediately; it might take several months to a year to secure a position.

➤ Make, use, and keep as many contacts as possible. You will need them for the next position, too.

➤ Take charge. Although you seek help from your school's counseling center and from friends, your job search is in your hands.

➤ Show what you can do. Potential employers can judge your worth better through internships than through interviews and better through interviews than through resumes.

➤ Plan alternative careers. At a minimum, if you are a doctoral student, plan routes leading to both academic and nonacademic careers.

➤ Do not pass up an entry-level position. It might be the right place to begin, and it is easier to get a job when you already have one.

How does a PHYSICIST . . .

Get to do TOXICOLOGY AND RISK ASSESSMENT?

After beginning her career as a physics major at Smith College, Resha Putzrath today is a self-employed consultant in toxicology and risk assessment. She reached her present position not by turning her back on physics, but by paying careful attention to her skills and preferences.

"In college," recalls Dr. Putzrath, "I imagined a career in high-energy physics. But I learned that career opportunities in high-energy physics were limited, and I realized that I was likely to be a junior member of a big team for a long time. That didn't suit me temperamentally."

Instead, she took advantage of each opportunity in her career path. Smith College acquired its first computer during her freshman year, allowing her to build early computing and mathematical skills. She made the most of summer jobs in biomedical laboratories. When it came time to plan graduate work, she saw that she could apply her love of mathematical physics to biologic systems. That led to a PhD in biophysics at the University of Rochester.

After her doctorate, she moved even farther from physics. An interest in membrane biology led her to postdoctoral study at Harvard Medical School. She then moved to the Harvard School of Public Health for a second postdoctoral

continued

appointment in toxicology and regulatory policy, where she discovered her current field.

Dr. Putzrath suggests to students that where they begin their career is not crucial—as long as they begin in earnest. "You must get very good training in *something*, or no one's interested in employing you for *anything*. But stay open to new opportunities. Today, it's very unlikely that you will have just one career."

She does caution against moving into self-employment too early. This is a step most easily taken when you have not only solid experience but also financial stability.

One way to broaden your abilities, increase your contacts, and reduce the isolation of working on your own is to form a cooperative association with other consultants. That allows you to share both work and information resources, which can be exchanged electronically even if your group members do not live in the same area.

➤ Do not lose heart. Although a lucky few might land positions before leaving school, finding a good job normally takes time and hard work.

Good career-planning centers are available at most universities for undergraduates, but not all departments and universities take seriously the challenge of helping graduate students to find employment.

Remember that the ultimate responsibility for finding a position must be yours. Even if your first position is not what you had imagined, it is a starting point. If you like what you are doing, there is nothing to stop you from finding—or creating—a job that is right for you.

Career Changes

It is important to recognize that a successful career in science or engineering requires continuous, life-long learning—not only in your own specialty, but also in adjacent fields. Your first permanent job will seldom be your last. In today's economy, workers in all fields should expect to change positions and even careers several times. The more skills you have picked up along the way, the more career opportunities you will have.

Career counselors often speak of career management. In part, this means knowing how to be prepared for change. It might be useful to ask yourself: What would I do if this field came to an end or I could no longer work in it? What do I want to do later in life?

A common obstacle to a successful career is to remain in an unproductive or unfulfilling job too long. Once you have decided that a position or even a career is not for you, find

Career Changes

Kim has worked hard to develop her career in environmental engineering. She completed a master's in geology, took a job, and managed to add an engineering degree by taking classes in the evenings. She has gained a position with a large consulting firm, where she links her expertise in groundwater movement with a good knowledge of regulatory policy.

However, after 5 years with the firm, she finds that she is more interested in the scientific aspects of her job than in the regulatory work. A friend suggests that she strike out on her own as a self-employed consultant.

➤ What should Kim consider before doing so?

➤ What are the advantages and disadvantages of self-employment?

See Appendix A for a discussion of this scenario.

another—even if it seems far from your original education or specialty. For example, many members of the prestigious National Academy of Engineering do not have engineering degrees; they began in other disciplines and responded to their own desire for change by moving into engineering. Career changes constitute tremendous opportunities. The sooner you make a constructive move, the better you will feel about yourself and the better you will look to the next employer.

Before attempting a career change, give careful thought to how you will present yourself. In an interview, describe what you can do not by categories—for example, most applicants in an academic position will be able to say that they can teach or conduct research—but by what you in particu-

How does an EXPERIMENTAL PSYCHOLOGIST . . .

Get to be a HUMAN FACTORS SPECIALIST?

Mary Carol Day's career began with a bachelor's in library science, which allowed her some financial flexibility, and a near-bachelor's in her real love, experimental psychology. By following her interests, she finds herself—several degrees and career changes later—happily (and unexpectedly) employed as technical manager of a Human Factors and User Interface Design group at AT&T Bell Laboratories. Her group designs human-computer interfaces, interactive voice response systems, and work processes and support systems that incorporate new technologies — making them as "user-friendly" as possible.

"Although most experimental psychologists have pursued careers vastly different from my own," says Dr. Day, "mine is not unique in the human factors community. Of more than 5,000 members of the Human Factors and Ergonomics Society, 39% have academic backgrounds in psychology and 9% in human factors. The field is growing, and it offers exciting opportunities in many areas."

Dr. Day describes herself as a "user advocate" who employs the tools of an experimental psychologist to optimize the usefulness of products and services. In doing so, she draws on an intensive and varied academic background.

continued

After earning her MA in experimental psychology at Florida State University and working in research at Yale and the City University of New York, she earned an EdD degree from the Human Development Program at Harvard. This was followed by a postdoctorate at the University of Pittsburgh and an assistant professorship in the psychology department of the University of Houston. There she conducted research on cognitive development from both Piagetian and information-processing perspectives.

"The decision to leave academe," she recalls, "was a difficult one, but it's one I don't regret. My work days are packed with varied and often unpredictable activities. We provide expertise on human capabilities and limitations, just as other project team members provide expertise on hardware and software. We conduct user needs and task analyses; we create and test user interfaces of new products. "A major challenge is to determine how much we can do, within demanding cost and time constraints, to ensure that the product meets users' needs and is easy to learn and use. This requires a broad understanding of human capabilities and a large toolbox of diverse methodologies for collecting valid and reliable data. In addition, we have to communicate well with people who may have very different perspectives from our own and to learn constantly about new technologies."

lar have done for your institution or group. For example, has management, teaching, or other experience led to excellent presentation skills? Have you led a task force or other group that accomplished its goals? Have you learned to help people to reach their goals? For further ideas, see sources in the bibliography, such as those published by the American Chemical Society and the Federation of American Societies of Experimental Biology (Kennedy 1995).

The best way to sustain a satisfying and productive career is to maintain your curiosity, openness, and yearning to know more. As long as you stay at the cutting edge of your field, your work will be meaningful and you will at least be considered for advancement. Industries have found that the most-efficient way to maintain a company's technical strength is not to hire replacements, but to support the continuing education of its experienced scientists and engineers. New techniques—including multimedia tools, distance learning, and computer-based learning—are making continuing education feasible and more effective (IEEE 1995).

A career change should never be made lightly, but with a sense that it builds on previous accomplishments and moves in a direction that you understand. How will the change benefit your career? You might find that most of your career changes occur fairly early; large directional changes become more difficult as you advance (Beynon 1993). In addition, it might be difficult to switch back to an academic career after time spent in industry, and vice versa. Ask others who have made similar switches in your field how difficult it was for them before switching rather than after. But the more knowledge and skills you accumulate, the more likely it is that your next move will be one that you—not someone else—have planned.

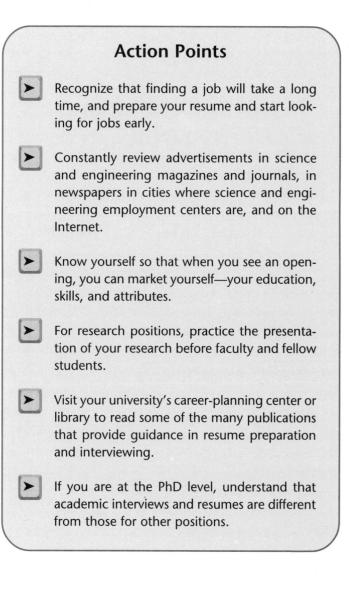

Action Points

➤ Recognize that finding a job will take a long time, and prepare your resume and start looking for jobs early.

➤ Constantly review advertisements in science and engineering magazines and journals, in newspapers in cities where science and engineering employment centers are, and on the Internet.

➤ Know yourself so that when you see an opening, you can market yourself—your education, skills, and attributes.

➤ For research positions, practice the presentation of your research before faculty and fellow students.

➤ Visit your university's career-planning center or library to read some of the many publications that provide guidance in resume preparation and interviewing.

➤ If you are at the PhD level, understand that academic interviews and resumes are different from those for other positions.

6

THE RESPONSIBILITY IS YOURS

Essential to the nature of both science and engineering is that they are both changing constantly. We can see that clearly by comparing what we see around us today with what we would have seen just a few years ago. We would not have seen a major new scientific field, like biotechnology; a major new engineering technique, like computer-aided design; a major new communication mechanism, like the Internet, or major new ways in which science and engineering can contribute to societal needs, like environmental engineering.

But change has its sobering consequences. For example, you might choose to enter a field that is "hot" today, only to find out that it is not so hot tomorrow. Life-long employment in any occupation has largely become a thing of the past. Even well-known tenure-track professors are being forced into early retirement; major industries are closing down their central research facilities.

What do those trends mean for you? Most importantly, they mean that any career you enter will be characterized by continual change and you will spend your career adapting to that change. In *Self-Renewal*, John Gardner writes:

> If we indoctrinate the young person in an elaborate set of fixed beliefs, we are ensuring his [or her] early obsolescence. The alternative is to develop skills, attitudes, habits of mind and the kinds of knowledge and understanding that will be the instruments of continuous change and growth . . . . Then we will have fashioned *a system that provides for its own continuous renewal* (1995).

What can you do to avoid obsolescence? You can acquire the life-long habit of watching for new fields to explore, new techniques to learn and use, and new societal needs to which you can contribute.

In the end, the responsibility of making your career successful is yours. The profiles you have seen throughout this guide provide excellent testimony to the fact that you can find interesting and valuable things to do, no matter where you begin. A successful career does not just happen; it has to be created. And you are the one to create it.

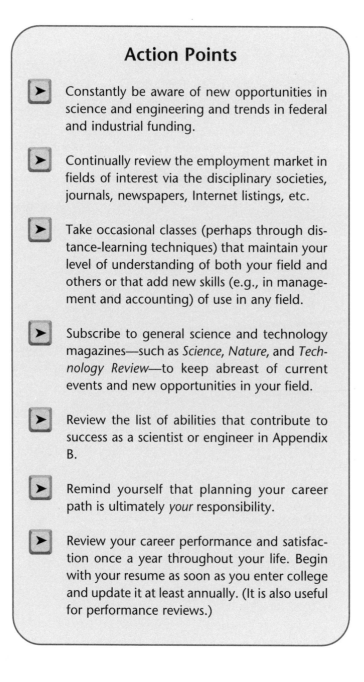

Action Points

➤ Constantly be aware of new opportunities in science and engineering and trends in federal and industrial funding.

➤ Continually review the employment market in fields of interest via the disciplinary societies, journals, newspapers, Internet listings, etc.

➤ Take occasional classes (perhaps through distance-learning techniques) that maintain your level of understanding of both your field and others or that add new skills (e.g., in management and accounting) of use in any field.

➤ Subscribe to general science and technology magazines—such as *Science, Nature,* and *Technology Review*—to keep abreast of current events and new opportunities in your field.

➤ Review the list of abilities that contribute to success as a scientist or engineer in Appendix B.

➤ Remind yourself that planning your career path is ultimately *your* responsibility.

➤ Review your career performance and satisfaction once a year throughout your life. Begin with your resume as soon as you enter college and update it at least annually. (It is also useful for performance reviews.)

BIBLIOGRAPHY

ACS (American Chemical Society)
> 1995 *The Interview Handbook.* Washington, DC: Department of Career Services, ACS.
>
> A thorough discussion of interviewing as well as self-evaluation and job assessment.
>
> *Targeting the Job Market.* Washington, DC: Department of Career Services, ACS.
>
> 1994 *Current Trends in Chemical Technology, Business, and Employment.* Washington, DC: Department of Career Services, ACS.
>
> *Directory of Graduate Research.* Washington, DC: Office of Professional Training, ACS.
>
> Published biannually.

Agre, Phil
> 1994 *Networking on the Network.*
>
> Available via the WWW at http://weber.ucsd.edu/~pagre/network. html

AIP (American Institute of Physics)
> 1995 *Career Opportunities: A Listing of Positions for People Trained in Physics and Related Fields.* College Park, MD: Division of Career Planning and Placement, AIP.
>
> A bimonthly listing of openings at academic, industrial, governmental, nonprofit, and other organizations.
>
> 1994 *Skills Used Frequently by Physics PhDs in Selected Employment Sectors.* College Park, MD: Division of Education and Employment Statistics, AIP.
>
> One-page graphic summary.

APA (American Psychological Association)
> 1996   *Psychology: Careers for the Twenty-first Century.* Washington, D.C.: APA.
>> A career guide for those who have academic training in psychology.

APS (American Physical Society) and AIP (American Institute of Physics)
> 1994   *Graduate Student Packet for Students in Physics.* Brian B. Schwartz, editor.
>> For physicists, some recent educational and employment statistics, tips on finding a job, and examples of career opportunities for PhD physicists, many of them in nontraditional positions.

Bailey, Nancy, and Arna Leavitt
> 1982   *Advancing by Degrees: Engineering B.S., M.S., Ph.D.* Prepared by the College of Engineering, University of Illinois at Urbana–Champaign. Washington DC: Engineering Deans Council, American Society for Engineering Education.
>> Brief but clear discussion on how to choose the best degree for your career in engineering.

Beveridge, W.I.B.
> 1950   *The Art of Scientific Investigation.* New York, NY: Vintage Books.

Beynon, Robert J.
> 1993   *Postgraduate Study in the Biological Sciences: A Researcher's Companion.* London, England: Portland Press Ltd.
>> While fairly traditional in orientation, this guide emphasizes the importance of planning at every stage in your academic career. ("Postgraduate" is British for "graduate.")

Bloom, Floyd, editor
> 1995   "Careers '95: The Future of the Ph.D.," *Science,* Vol. 270 (Oct. 6, 1995)

Bolles, Richard N.
> 1995   *The 1995 What Color Is Your Parachute?: A Practical Manual for Job-Hunters & Career-Changers.* Berkeley, CA: Ten Speed Press.
>> Although this popular guide is not specifically aimed at a scientific readership, most of its principles apply. Also, the author earned a physics degree from Harvard and studied chemical engineering at MIT.

Bundy, Alan, Ben du Boulay, Jim Howe, and Gordon Plotkin
> 1986   *The Researchers' Bible.* Technical Report DAI Teaching Paper No. 4, Edinburgh, Scotland: Department of Artificial Intelligence, University of Edinburgh.

CASS Recruitment Publications
> 1995   *Career Development Guide: Women in Engineering and Technology Edition.* Evanston, IL: Cass Communications, Inc.
>> Feature articles on such issues as women in technology, and salaries, relocation, and career opportunities for women.

CGS (Council of Graduate Schools)
> 1989   *Graduate School and You: A Guide for Prospective Graduate Students.* Washington, DC: CGS.

Detailed advice on how to decide why, whether, where, and when to go to graduate school, and how to finance a graduate education.

1990   *The Doctor of Philosophy Degree: A Policy Statement.* Washington, DC: CGS.
A brief overview of PhD education, from both the institution's and the student's viewpoint.

1990   *Research Student and Supervisor: An Approach to Good Supervisory Practice.* Washington, DC: CGS.
How careful planning and a good communication with your faculty adviser can lead to expeditious completion of PhD research and thesis. Adapted from a pamphlet published in Great Britain.

1991   *The Role and Nature of the Doctoral Dissertation: A Policy Statement.* Washington, DC: CGS.
Contains especially helpful sections on collaboration, the concept of "originality," and guidance for faculty advisers.

Chapman, David
1988   "How to Do Research at the MIT AI Lab." AI Working Paper 316. Cambridge, MA: Massachusetts Institute of Technology.

COSEPUP (Committee on Science, Engineering, and Public Policy)
1993   *Science, Technology, and the Federal Government: National Goals for a New Era.* Washington, DC: National Academy Press.

1995   *On Being a Scientist: Responsible Conduct in Research.* Washington, DC: National Academy Press.
An introduction to research ethics for beginning scientists and engineers, including case studies and ethical questions to ponder.

1995   *Reshaping the Graduate Education of Scientists and Engineers.* Washington, DC: National Academy Press.
A thorough discussion of many of the issues underlying this guide, such as the structure of graduate education and the changing needs of those who employ PhD scientists and engineers.

CPC (College Placement Council)
1994   *Catalog of Resources for Career Services and Employment Professionals.* Bethlehem, PA: CPC.
The CPC offers a variety of publications, statistical surveys, reports, and programs for universities and employers.

Dalton, G.W., and P.H. Thompson
1986   *Novations: Strategies for Career Management.* Glenview, IL: Scott, Foreman, and Co.
An excellent and detailed account of the expectations of employers and performance and skills of professional employees as the employee grows in his or her job function.

DesJardins, Marie
1994/   "How to Succeed in Graduate School: A Guide for Students and
1995   Advisors," *Crossroads, the Online ACM Student Magazine*
Available via WWW at http://info.acm.org/crossroads/xrds1-2/advice1.html

FASEB (Federation of American Societies for Experimental Biology)

1995   *CAREERS HardCopy*. Bethesda, MD: Federation of American Societies for Experimental Biology.

      Monthly, which in 1995 contained useful career advice by Irene Kennedy — "Prepare to Interview," "Show Employers What You Will Do" — and position listings.

Feibelman, Peter J.

1993   *A Ph.D. Is* **Not** *Enough! A Guide to Survival in Science.* Reading, MA: Addison-Wesley Publishing Co.

      The author's own painful missteps as a graduate student prompted him to offer this manual of "survival skills" for those planning a career in science or engineering.

Fiske, Peter S.

1996   *Beyond the Endless Frontier: A Practical Career Guide for Scientists.* Washington, DC: American Geophysical Union. Winter/Spring 1996.

Gardner, John W.

1995   *Self-Renewal: The Individual and the Innovative Society.* Revised edition. New York: W.W. Norton & Co.

      This is the book for the "rest of your career." Gardner, a former Secretary of Health, Education, and Welfare and founder of Common Cause, has excellent advice on nurturing your interests and creativity to stimulate growth throughout your working life.

Hall, Roberta M., and Bernice R. Sandler

1982   *The Classroom Climate: A Chilly One for Women.* Washington, DC: Association of American Colleges, Project on the Status and Education of Women.

1984   *Out of the Classroom: A Chilly Campus Climate for Women?* Washington, DC: Association of American Colleges, Project on the Status and Education of Women.

1986   *The Campus Climate Revisited: Chilly for Women Faculty, Administrators, and Graduate Students.* Washington, DC: Association of American Colleges, Project on the Status and Education of Women.

1983   *Academic Mentoring for Women Students and Faculty: A New Look at an Old Way to Get Ahead.* Washington, DC: Association of American Colleges, Project on the Status and Education of Women.

Hans, Sherrie, and Tanya Awabdy

1995   *Enhancing Graduate Training at UCSF.* San Francisco, CA: Program in the Biological Sciences, University of California at San Francisco.

      Summary of a career development symposium that was organized by graduate students.

IEEE (Institute of Electrical and Electronics Engineers, Inc.)

1995   *Industry 2000: Technical Vitality Through Continuing Education.* Piscataway NJ: IEEE.

A conference summary with valuable insights from both academic and industrial engineers on how to keep up with the rapid pace of technological change.

Professional Development: Where Do You Stand? A Message from Industry 2000. Video. Piscataway, NJ: Educational Activities Department, IEEE.

Jensen, David G.

1995 *Interview with "What Color Is Your Parachute?" Author Dick Bolles.* Sedona, AZ: Search Masters International.

Keirsey, D., and Marilyn Bates

1984 *Please Understand Me.* Del Mar, CA: Prometheus Nemesis Book Co.

Gives a very readable, popular introduction to the Meyer-Briggs approach to personality.

Kennedy, Irene

1995 Personal Communication with Deborah Stine, Washington DC, August 16, 1995.

Kirschner, Elizabeth M.

1995 "Nontraditional careers: Alternative careers lure chemists down a road less traveled." *Chemical & Engineering News* (Oct. 23): 51–55.

An argument that graduate schools should offer broader educational opportunities to students to prepare them for nonacademic as well as academic careers. Includes interviews with chemists and engineers holding nontraditional positions.

Landis, Raymond B.

1989 *An Academic Career: It Could Be for You: A Guide for Prospective Engineering Faculty Members.* Washington, DC: American Society for Engineering Education.

Is a faculty career for you? Tips on self-assessment and earning a doctorate.

LaPidus, Jules B., and Barbara Mishkin

1990 *Values and Ethics in the Graduate Education of Scientists.* Reprinted from: *Ethics and Higher Education,* William W. May, ed. Washington, DC: American Council on Education. Macmillan Publishing Company.

Useful advice for both students and faculty on dealing with ethical issues in research, with a helpful bibliography.

McKeachie, Wilbert J., editor

1994 *Teaching Tips: Strategies, Research, Theory for College and University Teachers,* Lexington, MA: D.C. Heath.

Medawar, P.B.

1979 *Advice to a Young Scientist.* Basic Books.

"I have tried to write the kind of book I myself should have liked to have read when I began research before most of my readers were born," writes Sir Peter, prefacing an account that is humorous, passionate, and as relevant today as when it was first published in 1979.

NACE (National Association of Colleges and Employers)
1996   *Job Choices in Science and Engineering,* 39th ed. Bethlehem, PA: NACE.

An A to Z listing of job opportunities at major American employers of scientists and engineers, plus feature articles.

NSF (National Science Foundation)
1989   "An NSF Study and Report About Women in Computing Research." *Computing Research News.*

OSEP (Office of Scientific and Engineering Personnel)
1995   *Research-Doctorate Programs in the United States: Continuity and Change.* Washington, DC: National Academy Press.

Peters, Robert L.
1992   *Getting What You Came For: The Smart Student's Guide to Earning a Master's or a Ph.D.* New York, NY: Noonday Press.

An excellent book-length guide that begins with the question of whether to go to graduate school and ends with tips on job hunting. Topics include choosing a school, thesis and thesis adviser, the master's versus the doctorate, building a reputation, proposing and writing the thesis, special issues for women and minority students, and forming a clear vision of your career. Full bibliography.

Peterson's/COG
1995   *MS/PhD: The Career Directory for Advanced Degree Engineers and Scientists.* Encino, CA: Peterson's/COG Publishing Group.

Phillips, Estelle M., and D.S. Pugh
1994   *How to Get a PhD: A Handbook for Students and Their Supervisors,* 2nd ed. Buckingham, England/Philadelphia, PA: Open University Press.

Discusses the doctorate experience (in Great Britain) not only from the student's point of view, but also from those of the faculty adviser and the university.

Presidential Task Force on the Study of Doctoral Education in Chemistry
1995   *Employment Patterns of Recent Doctorates in Chemistry: Institutional Perspectives and Imperatives for Change.* Washington, DC: American Chemical Society.

A summary of the study, including many figures and tables. Industry was found to be the largest employer of chemistry PhDs by a wide margin.

Rheingold, H.L.
1994   *The Psychologist's Guide to an Academic Career.* Washington, DC: American Psychological Association.

Rodman, Dorothy, Donald Bly, Fred Owens, and Ann-Claire Anderson.
1994   *Career Transitions for Chemists.* Washington, DC: Department of Career Services, American Chemical Society.

Saunders, J.H.
1974   *Careers in Industrial Research and Development.* New York, NY: Marcel Dekker.

Has a good discussion on personal attitudes and creative communication skills.

Sindermann, Carl J.
1987   *Survival Strategies for New Scientists.* New York, NY/London, England: Plenum Press.

The author argues that "doing good science is a worthwhile career objective, but there are *interpersonal strategies,* some quite complex, that enhance the pleasures of doing it." Illustrated by numerous case studies and bulleted lists of suggestions.

1985   *The Joy of Science.* New York: Plenum Press.

1982   *Winning the Games Scientists Play.* New York: Plenum Press.

Spertus, Ellen
1991   "Why are There so Few Female Computer Scientists?" MIT Artificial Intelligence Laboratory Technical Report 1315. Cambridge, MA: Massachusetts Institute of Technology.

Available on WWW at http://www.ai.mit.edu/people/ellens/Gender/pap/pap.html

Stern, Virginia, and Phyllis Dubois
1990   *You're in Charge,* Beth Goodrich, ed. Washington, DC: American Association for the Advancement of Science (AAAS).

A career-planning guide in science, mathematics, and engineering for college students with disabilities and the advocates and advisers who work with them.

Toth, Emily
1988   "Women in Academia," *The Academics' Handbook.* Durham, NC: Duke University Press.

Tobias, Sheila, Daryl E. Chubin, and Kevin Aylesworth
1995   *Rethinking Science as a Career: Perceptions and Realities in the Physical Sciences.* Tucson, AZ: Research Corp.

The authors examine career opportunities for scientists in the nonacademic sectors of society, and contend that "the nation needs a broad spectrum of professionals whose preparation includes a sound education in science."

University of Texas at Dallas
1995   *The Problem Solvers.* Doctor of Chemistry Program, University of Texas at Dallas.

Weisbrod, Glen, and Karen Hamilton
1994   *Globalization of Technology and the Economy: Implications for Mechanical Engineers: A Report on the Profession's External Environment.* New York: Committee on Issues Identification, American Society of Mechanical Engineers.

Contains an interesting section on new technologies and business priorities, including energy generation, industrial energy efficiency, and transportation.

APPENDIXES

DISCUSSION OF SCENARIOS

Approaching a Career

Now is the time for Ellie to think carefully about her next steps. Is she sure that she will enjoy working with students? She might benefit from some form of practice teaching either as a tutor or as a volunteer in a community service project for high-school students or adults. Taking the Graduate Record Exam might let her gauge her aptitude for doing advanced coursework, although it can tell her little about other aspects of graduate education. It is unusual for a high-school teacher to desire the rigorous work demanded of a master's or PhD in mathematics. However, some PhDs have found rewarding careers in teaching at the pre-college level, and many high schools and community colleges explicitly want to hire teachers at the master's level or even PhD level (in magnet schools, for example).

If she has doubts about whether teaching is for her, this is the time to investigate alternatives. She might take courses in disciplines in which her interest in mathematics would be an asset, such as engineering, accounting, or biology. She might take a summer job in the private sector (with an actuarial or accounting firm, for example) to familiarize herself with other mathematics-related careers. As science and technology become more pervasive in our culture, mathematicians are increasingly in demand in positions outside academia, including environmental work, health science, business, finance, and banking.

If she decides on high-school teaching, she will benefit from a master's degree for the best chances of career advancement. She will also need her state's teaching certificate; many states have alternative certification programs for those with graduate degrees, allowing people to teach and obtain certification at the same time.

Evaluating Yourself

Frank has two questions to answer: What opportunities are available to him as a chemist? How do his personality and abilities match with these opportunities?

In thinking about the profession of chemistry, he can begin his search with the career counselor in his college, who will have advice about graduate study and potential careers. He should also get in touch with the American Chemical Society (which has local sections) and ask for useful materials on career planning. He should ask both sources for names of professionals whom he might talk to. He should watch for local disciplinary meetings and seek out people there.

To understand his own personal needs better, Frank should review his personal life and experience. He might make a list of his accomplishments and weigh them against his shortcomings. What can such a list tell him about the employment that he is best suited to? His counseling office will probably offer a personality or aptitude test. Although the results of the test might be helpful, he might find even more benefit from just thinking about the questions asked on the test.

Frank should attempt an evaluation of who he is and what he wants. Does he thrive on challenge, competition, and problem-solving? If so, he might prefer a position in which initiative is prized. Does he place high value on security, benefits, and long-term security? If so, he might do well in a less-challenging but more-stable position. The better he knows himself, the sounder will be his decision.

Communication Skills

If such skills are important to her, there are many opportunities to develop them without adding extra courses. For example, to build communication and group skills, Lee could join a graduate-student seminar group. Organizing one would also help to strengthen her leadership and group skills. She could join a disciplinary society and take on the responsibilities of organizing workshops and planning meetings. Making contacts, initiating plans, and making public announcements will all be helpful. Joining a Toastmaster's Club could help to strengthen communication and public-speaking skills.

To better understand the culture and work style of industry, she could try to arrange off-campus, for-credit internships to take the place of courses. She might find an off-campus adviser as well. She could practice explaining the importance of her field to off-campus or civic groups.

Team Skills

It is true that a dedicated researcher can have a career as an independent scholar. But all disciplines, including mathematics, are becoming more team-oriented.

Graduate school provides many opportunities to learn to work cooperatively—for those willing to seize them. Perhaps with the help of a friend or counselor, Howard should make an effort to interact with students in adjacent disciplines, such as physics, engineering, biology, and computer science. He could organize projects or groups, look for intellectual "edges" where his work meets the work of others, and make conscious efforts to participate in discussions, seminars, and workshops.

Deciding Whether to Attend Graduate School

By moving directly into a job, Chris might very well satisfy her desires to earn an adequate income, to live close to home, and to have a rewarding career.

If, after a few years, her interest in further study is rekindled, she will likely have gained valuable skills and a realistic perspective on her field. She will have had a break from school, which often proves refreshing. She might also be able to earn a master's degree while working, most likely with her employer's support.

However, after a few years off campus, it could be difficult to leave the job and to regain momentum for a PhD. She would have to shift from receiving a good salary to living on a student scholarship or loan funds. She would have lost touch with some of her academic material in a field that is changing rapidly.

It is important for Chris to consider the eventual shape of her career. An advanced degree will allow her to move up the career ladder and attain higher levels of responsibility and salary.

If she does not want to move, it is sometimes possible to obtain adequate schooling at a smaller institution near one's home. Regional schools often specialize in subfields that are attractive to potential employers and provide an excellent path to an industrial position. A good regional university can often provide the management, organizational, or financial skills needed for advancement.

Choosing a Degree

Wesley's social skills and love of teaching suggest a natural path toward education. He needs to think about what level of teaching suits him best. If he stops at a master's in chemistry, his best option might be to teach at the junior-college or high-school level; he could also work as a technician in a chemical company. If he hopes to do research or to teach at the university level, he will need a PhD and probably postdoctoral experience.

His good communication skills are highly valued in the private sector. He might choose to go on to the PhD and broaden its value through an internship with industry. This might lead to a career in R&D, applications, marketing, or sales. Corporations value people who can explain complex subjects to customers and co-workers in other disciplines. Wesley might do well to seek out an adviser in industry.

His adviser's reluctance to discuss the full range of career options is a serious drawback. An adviser's support is invaluable in gaining perspective on one's career and in making career contacts. Wesley should find another adviser or seek a second adviser who can help him.

The Adviser–Student Relationship

Fernando should make every effort to speak with his adviser; misunderstandings are common in the hectic environment of graduate school. If his attempt fails, he should consult the head of the graduate program, whose job it is to be the liaison between students and faculty. If this fails, he might talk with his department chair.

Is this problem his adviser's fault, or is he himself doing something that contributes to a poor relationship? This kind of difficulty is a good argument for taking great care in choosing an adviser.

If Fernando is truly blocked, he might need to find another adviser. There are risks to this step: he might not find one in his field, he might lose time in reshaping his career, and he might lose financial support. But unless he is nearly finished with his research, selecting another adviser is probably preferable to continued unhappiness and lack of progress.

Choosing a Research Topic

It is not uncommon to shift the focus of thesis research, but there must be *some* focus. Without it, Henry faces several grave dangers, such as repeating what someone else has already done, losing his way amid the immensity of his subject, or trying to do the work of an entire career in a brief time.

Most advisers can help to prevent these mistakes, but

only if lines of communication are open. This communication is a responsibility shared by Henry and his adviser.

At this point, Henry can only make the best of a poor situation. To begin with, he should seek out opinions from the other members of his research committee. He has already done considerable research; with their guidance, he should be able to put together a decent (if not first-class) dissertation. He might have hoped for better, but obtaining a PhD at least provides a tangible return on his investment of effort.

Finding a Job

Carol should start immediately to learn what she can about corporate culture. She should use her contacts and friends to obtain coaching from biotechnology experts and others familiar with private-company values.

She should also sharpen her communication skills by working with friends, taking classes, or hiring a tutor. Disciplinary groups are especially helpful. They often have listings of job-opening services that help to match employers looking for employees with members looking for jobs and a variety of written guidance material, including resume, interview, and job-search guides.

Scientists and engineers who work for industry are commonly called on to work in teams, to follow products beyond the laboratory, and to interact with customers or co-workers in other disciplines. Therefore, Carol would benefit from good skills in communication, teamwork, and leadership. Industry places more emphasis on timeliness, goals, and cost control than there is in academic research. Even a brief experience in an industrial laboratory during a summer or off-campus internship might have prepared Carol for these expectations.

Carol should not give up easily. It takes work and time to find a job; a search commonly lasts 6-12 months.

Career Changes

Self-employment requires considerable maturity and experience. Kim should assess her position before leaving her firm: Has she become expert in her field? Does she have enough contacts to bring her steady employment? Does she have the financial stability to endure the months when her income is below average? One rule of thumb is to have a year's income in the bank before venturing out.

Some advantages of self-employment are increased flexibility, responsibility, and choice. On the other side of the coin, Kim will lose the infrastructure, advisers, and teamwork that supported her activities in the firm. Unless she is part of a group, she will also have to deal with the isolation factor—doing without the personal interaction, intensity, and (in most cases) fun of the workplace. She should ask herself whether she has the perseverance and self-reliance to do without those and whether independence is truly important to her. If the answers are positive, self-employment could offer an unparalleled opportunity for growth.

SKILLS AND ATTRIBUTES THAT CONTRIBUTE TO SUCCESS IN SCIENCE OR ENGINEERING

Ellis B. Cowling

Graduate education is a process by which individual master's-degree and doctoral-degree candidates develop into scientists, engineers, or other professionals who are capable of independent research, development, and application activities of high quality. Progress is achieved by the student with the guidance of an advisory committee of faculty drawn from the university department(s) in which the student is pursuing the degree. Because the career path of every student is unique, the counsel that any particular student receives from faculty advisers should be tailored to fit each individual student's unique set of developing skills, abilities, personality characteristics, and career aspirations. This counsel should also be distinctive and appropriate to the degree for which the student is a candidate.

The challenge for students is to know themselves well enough to

- Understand their particular strengths and weaknesses as aspiring scientists, engineers, or other professionals.

• Be wise in the selection of their major professor and other members of an advisory committee who can help them realize as much as possible of their potential.

• Be persistent in seeking to maximize their progress in realizing as much as possible of their potential.

The challenge for faculty advisers is to get to know the student well enough to understand the present stage of development of the student's abilities and his or her potential for improvement. The committee also must have the wisdom to know how to help the student to achieve something approaching his or her full potential.

The objective of all interactions between the student, the major professor, and other members of the advisory committee should be to maintain abilities in which the student already has developed strength while helping him or her to increase abilities that are not yet developed fully.

The following lists of abilities have been prepared as a guide to the interactive processes through which individual graduate students and advisory committees can work together to meet the goal of creating a new scientist, engineer, or professional of high quality.

Skills and Attributes that Contribute to a Successful Career as a Scientist, Engineer, Scholar, or Professional

Intellectual Skills

1. Honesty
2. Curiosity
3. Discrimination—ability to distinguish what is important from what is trivial
4. Imagination and creativity
5. Common sense
6. Objectivity
7. Intuition
8. Skill in observation of natural, technical, or social phenomena
9. Systematic problem-solving
10. A good memory
11. Capacity for logical reasoning, including abstract and theoretical reasoning
12. Capacity to draw logical inferences from observational and experimental data
13. Ability to conceive an explanatory hypothesis and design critical tests to evaluate it

Communication Skills

1. Capacity to retrieve information from published sources
2. Skill in learning by interview methods
3. Capacity to communicate in writing
4. Capacity to communicate orally
5. Skill in use of computers and other information-processing devices
6. Skill in graphic display of information and ideas

Personality Characteristics

1. Maturity
2. Motivation and drive
3. Self-confidence
4. Dependability
5. Independence
6. Empathy
7. Capacity to work effectively with superiors, peers, and subordinates
8. Initiative and sense of responsibility
9. Capacity for objective self-criticism
10. Leadership and management skills

Habits of Work

1. Efficiency in the use of time
2. Persistence—ability to see things through to completion
3. Capacity for sustained intellectual and physical work
4. Orderliness
5. Ability to meet deadlines

Mechanical Skills

1. Manual dexterity
2. Skill in the development, selection, and use of appropriate scientific, engineering, or artistic apparatus, machines, and models